# Don't Laugh! You'll Wake the Dog!

## Humorous Musings on
## All Things Funny and Furry and Fuzzy

Leigh Anne Jasheway

Comedy Workout Publishing

Eugene, OR

*To Megan ~ may you laugh heartily!*

*Leigh Anne*

**Also by Leigh Anne Jasheway:**

101 Comedy Games for Children and Grown-Ups

Are You Playing with Me?

Bedtime Stories for Dogs

Bedtime Stories for Cats

Confessions of a Semi-Natural Woman

Date Me, Date My Dog

Don't Get Mad, Get Funny

Give Me a Break

How'd All These Ping Pong Balls Get in My Bag?!

If I Was a Dog, I'd be a Better Person

I'm Not Getting Older (I'm Getting Better at Denial)

Laugh Lines are Beautiful

Laugh Track and Field

Life is Funny

Not Guilty by Reason of Menopause

The Rules for Dogs

The Rules for Cats

Serious Side Effects

Yoga for Your Funny Bone

*Don't Laugh! You'll Wake the Dog*

## Preface

Some people like reading books that depress them because by comparison their lives look simple and wonderful. I started life off this way. I was a Brothers Karamazov/Dr. Zhivago/The Bell Jar kind of a girl when I was young. Had there been such a category in my high school yearbook, I would have been voted most likely to depress people.

But something changed along the way. In my early 30s, I realized I preferred the sounds of laughter to the sounds of crying.     The ability to turn life's little stressors and its big disasters into something that can make people—including myself—laugh is the closest I'm ever going to come to having a superpower, so I'd better use it. Otherwise, the Organization Of Super Heroes (OOSH) will revoke my license and my spandex outfit.

As I write this, it's been 21 years since I quit my day job, packed up kit, caboodle, and wiener dogs, moved across country and decided to see if it might be possible to forge some kind of career out of being funny. I discovered along the way that it was possible as long as I redefined "career," "success" and "appropriate business wear." I've won a few prizes (including the prestigious Erma Bombeck Humor Writing Award), gone a few fancy places, and met a few of my idols. But more important than all of that, I've giggled so much I now have laugh lines on my pancreas.

Thank you to everyone who has been part of this journey—from my teachers and mentors, to people who hired me to write for them despite their first instincts not to, to anyone who has ever knocked on the stall door in a public bathroom and told me I've made them laugh. This may be why I have a nervous bladder, but it's also the reason I no longer sit in my closet reading Edgar Alan Poe by flashlight. With my eyesight these days, that's a good thing.

**Not Top Dog**

I have been under dachshund management for 28 years. That's 196 in dog years. Facebook hadn't been invented. Justin Bieber hadn't been born. Teenagers said *groovy* instead of *awesome*. People had not yet evolved to have a hunch in their back so that they could walk around while watching funny videos on their cell phones.

As with many organizations, ours has been through some change lately. A new supervisor joined the ranks in December and we're all trying to renegotiate our contracts. Justin continues to be the top dog, in charge of security (which includes staring out the window, chasing away squirrels and doing "security checks" on visitors.) He will also search purses and backpacks if he has just cause to believe cookies could be involved. Naturally, Justin is also the director of meal scheduling. His talent for waking up at 4 a.m. and standing on my chest until I awaken from lack of oxygen assures that breakfast is always served before dawn.

One step down the organizational chart is Penny, our human-canine relations director who makes sure that once visitors have been approved at the door and had their belongings examined, they feel loved and needed. She accomplishes this by crawling into their laps and demanding belly rubs for the entire time of their visit. Penny is also charged with maintaining a dress code that does NOT include a pink puffy coat with fake fur at the collar because it makes her look fat.

The latest addition to our group is Watson, who has quickly shown his talents and been assigned to trash disposal, landscape redesign and professional development and training. The latter includes teaching me, the only non-managerial employee how to get him to let go of a squeak toy he's been ripping apart by chasing him around my desk for hours at time. Word is that Watson may also be assigned the company's overall fitness program as well. I've lost 3 pounds since he arrived, so it's a role he'll be good at.

It's not easy reporting to three bosses. It's not that I've ever been the alpha dog, but I'm certain that I'm now the zamboni dog. Like any employee in this position, most of my time is spent making sure things around the office run smoothly. I schedule my employers' appointments, clean up their messes and lie for them. *"I'm sorry Justin missed his therapy session; he was busy, uh, determining whether enough sunlight hits the sofa to warrant installing solar panels on the roof."*

Watson, however, has added new responsibilities to my job description. While Justin and Penny use a system of ramps to get onto the sofa and into bed, Watson insists on being bribed with a cookie to do so. You'd think there'd be jealousy as a result, but Justin and Penny are happy that occasionally they now get extra cookies. This is one of the reasons we now need a company-wide fitness program.

If you've ever had to maintain peace among your superiors, you know how I feel when taking my doggy bosses for their morning constitutional. I am only one person with only two arms, so two dogs must be leashed together, meaning they must work at a team at all times or the whole system breaks down. Because he is CEO, we wouldn't think to ask Justin to give up his personal freedom, so Penny and Watson spend most of the time trying to be the lead dog. Watson may be almost twice her size, but Penny is wily and cute, which can get you far in both the business world and while sniffing your way around the block.

Needless to say, at day's end, we all sleep well. Watson somehow manages to take up half the king size bed, while Justin and Penny prefer sleeping on top of me to make sure I will be there in the morning to open and close and open and close and open and close the sliding door to the back yard. They've determined that the best way to maintain a high rate of employee retention is to never let me out of their sight.

As you might imagine, I am a very busy employee, but there are many perks to the job. As many of you probably do, I laugh at my bosses... a lot. Just yesterday, Justin and Watson attempted to use the doggy door at the same time and got stuck. Penny and I giggled like school girls. A few weeks ago a squirrel chased Justin around the yard and uncontrollable snickers erupted.

Every day at 11 a.m., we have a mini-carrot break (because coffee and donuts are not good for canines or hyper employees). For a few minutes as we snack, we forget who is superior to whom. It's also great that every day is casual day around here.

The best part of my job is that when I have to leave the office, say to make a run for dog cookies or squeak toys, upon my return, my bosses are extremely happy to see me. Sure all my outfits are covered with paw prints, but if you're going to be walked on by your superiors, it helps if they're all wagging their tails and licking your face.

Oops, I've got to go now. Watson wants on the couch, so I'll need to get some cookies.

## Don't Sit Down!

It all started with a pain in my backside, a pain that was caused by… are you ready for this?… sitting. That's right, I hurt myself sitting. Of all the injuries you can sustain in life, pulling a muscle in your butt from perching on a chair has to rank right up there with the most humiliating. Especially when you have to explain it to a physical therapist who obviously lifts hybrid cars on her lunch break to keep in shape.

It's nice to have a medical diagnosis for my pain (a pulled ischial tuberosity), but I could have done without our conversation. It went something like this:

> PT: Why don't you have a seat on the table?
> Me: Okay.

I sit down. At least that's what I think I'm doing.

> PT: Oh no. That's all wrong.
> Me: Yeah, I know, I slouch a little when I sit. I've been working on it (mostly by visualizing myself sitting straighter, not by actually doing anything about it).
> PT: Yeah, the way you sit isn't good. But the way you go from standing to sitting is all wrong. Stand up.

I do, with some trepidation.

> PT: Wow. You don't stand up correctly either. No wonder your butt hurts. I'm surprised you can walk at all.

She then proceeded to show me how to sit down. Apparently, I should bend at the hip joint first as if a large man with a black belt in martial arts has just karate chopped me at the pelvis. Then and only then should I lower my butt down to the seat. The same action is supposed to happen when standing up, only in reverse. We practiced this for 10 minutes. Her bill was $300 for an hour, so I spent $50 learning how to sit down and stand up. You'd think that at the ripe age of mumbledy-something, I'd have figured out the basics in life such as sitting, standing, and not paying $300 an hour to have a physical therapist make me feel bad about myself. But nooo... Apparently I have a really long learning curve.

After the PT thought I had progressed, I got to demonstrate standing in place for her. Apparently I didn't have that down either.

PT: Your right hip is way in front of your left hip. This isn't good.

I thought she was going to tell me I should step twice with my right leg for each step on the left just to even up the difference, but instead she dug her thumb into my hip joint so deeply I believe police could identify her from the print she left on my femur. I'm not sure what she was hoping to accomplish – it could have been some form of acupressure or maybe she spotted a spider on me and felt compelled to squish it.

Afterward, I still had a pain in my butt and my right hip hurt too. And I was afraid to either sit or stand, for fear someone would judge me. I began to worry about other basic life skills such as chewing and sleeping too. What if I also did those wrong?

When I got home, I tentatively sat down, using the karate chop image to make sure I did so correctly. To take my mind off the pain, I opened up the newspaper and noticed a story with the headline "Experts Say Sitting Can Kill You." I jumped up so quickly, I almost gave myself whiplash.

According to the article (which I read standing up while trying to make sure my hips were even), even if you exercise regularly, spending the majority of your day sitting down can lead to obesity, high blood sugar, and higher risk of death. The study didn't say anything about pulling a muscle. I made a mental note to call the scientists and let them know about their omission.

Needless to say, now I'm really worried. I don't know how to sit properly and now I find out I should avoid it at all costs. But I also don't stand properly. As far as I know, the only other body position I'm capable of maintaining for any period of time is lying down. But I can't imagine being able to write while supine, especially considering the fact that when I lie down for more than a few minutes, my dogs drape themselves over parts of my body. There are mornings I wake up unable to walk because my legs are both completely asleep from lack of blood flow during the night.

I only have two options, I guess. I can invest $2,000 or more in a treadmill desk because as far as I know my walking is okay as long as I don't stand still. Ever. Or I could invest in a harness and pulley contraption and spend my days suspended from the ceiling. I remember Dolly Parton, Jane Fonda, and Lily Tomlin kept their boss Dabney Coleman in one of those things in the old movie, *9 to 5*. Surely I could hang from the ceiling error-free.

The only problem I have now (besides pain in my rear end, a sore hip, and fear of sitting or standing) is that I'm afraid to Google "leather harness" to see where I can get one. Treadmill desk it is then.

**In Praise of Granny Panties**

I took a friend lingerie shopping recently. She's been married for two years now and it's time for her to switch to comfortable undies. Let's be truthful here – if you're still wearing thong panties, you're probably still dating. I have six pairs of thongs. I use them to stake up my tomatoes in summer. In the winter, I make little hammocks for hamsters that I sell on Etsy.

Eventually there comes a time in every woman's life when the words "Granny Panties" no longer strike fear in a her heart. This is at the point when she starts calculating just how much of her time she spends digging her sexy underwear out from places it doesn't belong. And wonders how many times she's been caught doing just that on camera and then has to spend all night checking YouTube to be sure.

What has always struck me as odd is that men have no hesitation referring to any type of underwear that covers a woman's backside as "Granny Panties," but they can pull their tidy whities up to their underarms and parade around the house thinking they look like George Clooney or Channing Tatum or whoever is hot these days.

I took my friend to Victoria's Secret. She thought she could get something cute and comfy there. Yeah, right! Personally, I think Victoria should have kept her secret to herself and we'd all be a lot better off. It's her fault men think that all women should dress like supermodels, who often parade around in their matching bra and panties at the beach with a come-hither look on their face. In all my years, I have never felt the urge to wade into the surf in nothing but my skivvies. My bra and panties almost never match either. Heck, my boobs don't even match – I have a B cup and a C cup. The left one's an overachiever. And I must admit my "come hither" look is really more of a "she needs her meds adjusted" look.

There are many things you can buy to wear underneath it all that you really shouldn't. For example, anything with pearls where the backside should be. Now don't get me wrong – I'm originally from the south and I enjoy a good string of pearls. Grace Kelly wore pearls, for gosh sakes. Just not where the sun don't shine.

You just know the idea of a pearl thong had to come from the testosterone-laden brain of a guy during halftime. No woman would willingly create an idea so heinous. Because while a pearl thong might look good on a supermodel with no cellulite and legs that actually do go all the way to there, the rest of us are not so lucky. Real women have real needs. Like sitting down. That's not going to happen in one of those. Nor is walking. You'd take a few steps and that sucker would ride up so high you'd have to shake your leg like an epileptic horse to adjust yourself.

Why can't we women just be happy with underwear that fits well, doesn't bunch up, and costs less than a tank of gas? 99% of the time our undies are hidden under our clothes, and the other 1%, well, he's over there in the same pair of briefs he's been wearing since high school thinking he's all that. I think our best bet is to save the $135 a pair of pearl thong panties would set us back and spend it on 20 new boxers for the guy in your life. Believe me, you'll be glad you did.

**Puppy Love**

I first fell head over heels in love in 1984. He had red hair and brown eyes and my heart skipped a beat at the mere thought of him (and that was well before my mitral valve issues). Two weeks later, I fell in love with his brother too – a dark-haired hunk whose zest for life was infectious.

So I took them both home.

We were quite a threesome, my first two dachshunds – Copper and Slate – and I. And in the years since there have been four more – Maddy Lou, Justin, Penny, and Watson – about whom I have felt just as giddy. So, in honor of Valentine's Day, I thought I'd write about true love of the canine variety. Puppy love, if you will.

I see some of you rolling your eyes and insisting that Valentine's Day is supposed to be a celebration of romantic love. But according to an online dictionary (we know it must be true if it's online, right?), "romantic love" is when the chemicals in your brain kick in and you experience an emotional high, exhilaration, and elation whenever you and your love are together. That doesn't just happen between humans. I dare any scientist to take a blood sample to see just what chemicals (besides caffeine and chocolate) are surging through my veins when I come home and my wiener dogs wag their tails and do their "We Love Her So Much We'd Almost Even Give up Chasing Squirrels for Her" dance.

It is important to show our love to the humans we can't live without by buying them aftershave and 47-lb. heart-shaped boxes of chocolate, two-thirds of which have icky pink cream fillings that make us gag a little. And we should do that even if we're irritated with them because the true love chemicals and the willingness to wear a body shaper and heels have worn off.

But why not also celebrate interspecies love during Valentine's Day? Talk about unconditional – nothing my dogs do truly irritates me. Penny can piddle on the floor right in front of me because it's raining outside and she prefers to be dry, and as hard as I try to be annoyed with her, I am still overwhelmed by the same rush of love I felt that day I adopted her from a rescue organization and she crawled into my lap as if to say, "Well, it took you long enough!" Justin can stand on my trachea at 4:07 a.m. because he's decided that despite what the clock says, it really must be time for breakfast. As sleepy and grumpy as I usually am at that time of morning, I'll still call him "Dog Muffin" as I'm serving up his kibble in the wee dark hours of the morning. (By the way, standing on someone's trachea is an excellent way to wake them up. As long as you're under 25-lbs.) And Watson can insist I lift him onto the sofa even though he just jumped down seconds ago because he was sure I was thinking about getting him a mini-carrot from the 'fridge. He's still my little Clydesdale.

It is difficult, however, to find the perfect way to celebrate Valentine's Day with a four-footed friend. Even I have a hard time – and I once threw Maddy Lou a debutante party to which my best friend Rhonda wore a hoop skirt and presented Maddy Lou with her own bone china tea set which I still have in my hope chest. I can't imagine how much trouble it is for those of you who don't have my party-organizing skills.

A candlelit Valentine's Day dinner for dogs is a little over the top. Not to mention that I really shouldn't be allowed around an open flame. Or a stove. Greeting card companies make Valentine's Day cards from the dog ("I love you… despite the fact that you feed me all your peas and then blame me for the consequences"), but not TO them. That's a darn shame if you ask me. And although I've been known to dress my dogs up coats and sweaters, Valentine's Day doggy lingerie is a little too kinky even for me.

There are boutique pet stores in town that carry carob-coated doggy treats shaped like little hearts, but I know what my dogs really want – besides some table scraps that don't consist primarily of tofu and brown rice. What they truly want for Valentine's Day is for me to sit on the couch for twelve straight hours without moving a muscle – no laughing, no blinking, and no breathing so deeply that my stomach goes up and down and interrupts their naps. They want me to be their Valentine's hostage. And that's what they're going to get. I've been practicing motionlessness and shallow breathing for a week now and will have it down pat by the big day.

Happy Valentine's Day to you and all your loves, no matter what species!

**Flirt Your Way to Better Health**

Want to do something healthy and fun? According to researchers, you can get a boost to both your immune system and your self-confidence if you flirt.

Having grown bored of my elliptical trainer and kale smoothies, I'm willing to give flirting a go, but to be truthful the whole activity confuses me. Maybe I've spent too much time in the company of dogs. When a dog is interested in me, I pick up on those signals right away—tail wagging, tongue hanging out, excess salivation, and paws either on my knees or shoulders depending upon the size of the hound and whether I've already been wrestled to the floor. If a human flirted in that manner, I'm fairly certain a call to 911 would be called for.

When I'm in the non-canine world, I'm never certain if or whether I'm being flirted with. A few months ago I was out on the town with a friend when a man came over to our table and stood there chatting with me for ten minutes, occasionally flipping his ponytail away from his face. Afterward, I asked my friend whether she thought he was flirting with me. "Well, he did have his hand on your knee at one point, so yeah," she replied, shaking her head at my obtuseness. I thought he'd just lost his balance. At his age, that might have been the case.

Even if you're married or in a long-term relationship, researchers say you will get health benefits of making googly—as opposed to Google—eyes with your significant other. So what have you got to lose? But before you or I start a health-boosting flirting program, perhaps a brief review of what is and isn't considered flirtatious is in order for all of us. If this saves anyone from ending up as the subject of a viral video, my work here will be done.

The hair flip – This move makes the top of many lists of flirting tips, but the activity is usually meant  for women. Clearly my male flirter had read the wrong list, or he just had a rambunctious ponytail that would not stay in place. When flipping you hair, be sure not to do so with such force that you forget who you are (this tip may come in handy for over-50-flirters).

<u>Eye contact</u> – This is important in every human interaction, but in flirting there is a fine line between trying to catch someone's attention and giving him or her the creeps. It's important to remember to blink and to know when to look away, for example, when the person you're flirting with has actually been out of the room for more than 30 minutes.

<u>Smiles and laughter</u> – Apparently a nice smile and ready laughter are sure signs of trying to connect intimately with someone. Okay, I see now why men often think I'm trying to lead them on, but the truth is I laugh at lot, thus the laugh lines on my, well, everything. Please don't think I'm toying with you if I laugh at all your jokes then leave the room; I was born this way. For those of you who don't suffer from LSD (Laughter Surplus Disorder), laugh appropriately and not maniacally and you should be safe.

<u>Touch</u> – As with eye contact, touch is an important way to establish a bond with someone, but it's important to know the limits. If you just met someone for example, try a subtle approach to physical contact—pick a piece of lint off her shoulder or adjust his tie. You are also encouraged to pat someone down should he or she set a sleeve on fire, but you may not light the match.

In the research I did for this article, I read a how-to-flirt article for younger people and one aimed at flirters over 50 and found that there are some substantial differences. I will share these with you here so that you don't accidentally flirt outside your age group. Younger people are encouraged to be klutzy. That's a flirting tip? For me, it's more of a lifestyle. All those times I walked into plate glass doors, smacked waiters in the mouth as I talked with my hands or tripped over my own feet and or fell in guys' laps, those are considered flirtatious? Who knew?

Younger people are also encouraged to, "hit on the wingman. " People over 50 think a wingman is a hockey position and have no idea why someone would try to make eye contact with or smile at a goalie while the puck is coming straight for his head. That would be dangerous, right?

Those of us who have been around the block a time or 400 are told to use etiquette to our advantage – pull out a chair, open a door, or write thank you notes to your friends while flirting. The tips also suggest we be sexy but subtle: Licking your lips is out, but batting your eyelashes is okay, as long as you don't overdo it because as you know every woman over 35 has insufficient eyelashes and you wouldn't want to litter the table with those that remain. If you're a guy who is losing his hair, avoid hair flipping for the same reason.

Well, now we know the rules, so let's get out there and boost our immune systems. I promise not set your sleeve on fire if you promise not to drool on my shoulder.

**Now That's Attractive**

An amazing scientific discovery was recently announced in the coupon section of my newspaper. For decades women everywhere have been hoping and praying for this kind of breakthrough and it's finally here. Teams of scientific researchers working day and night in musty basements across the country have finally harnessed the technology to develop – wait for it – magnetized panties that can instantly take off 10-15 pounds!

Don't you feel better already?

Now I'm not one to pooh-pooh anything that can make my hips and backside look like they did when I was younger, thinner, and less likely to obey the law of gravity, but magnets in our underpants? Really?

And it's not just one or two magnets either – according to the ad, uh, study, each pair of "magnetic slimming panties" contains hundreds of the things. For the skeptical reader, there's a close-up photo to prove just how many of them are woven into the fabric. The number of magnets isn't what causes my skepticism, however. It's how they supposedly "make the derriere more shapely, flatten the tummy and smooth the hips." These are all fine goals, but how is it done? Do the magnets align all the fat cells to point north so that when viewed from the east or west you look thinner? (I use a trick like this myself. I'm much thinner when viewed from the side while leaning against a larger object such as Jupiter. I don't need magnets for that, however.)

Maybe with all these powerful magnets in your undies, you will be attracted to large metal surfaces such passing automobiles and all the running you have to do you keep up with moving vehicles, not to mention the strength required to peel yourself off the bumper, will burn so many calories that you actually lose weight. On the other hand, you could find yourself stuck to the refrigerator and heaven knows that's not a good place for anyone trying to appear slimmer and more toned.

I have had experience with magnets, although never in my undergarments. I once had carpal tunnel problems and my chiropractor at the time recommended that I wear magnets taped to my little fingers to improve my circulation and reduce my pain. Neither of those things happened. Instead I had the distinct feeling that bolts of electricity were coursing down my arms and shooting out my fingertips. It's the closest I've come to having a superpower and I can truthfully say I wasn't that fond of the experience. There was no instruction manual telling me how I was supposed to use my electrical powers for good not evil. Also I didn't look that great in the Spandex superhero outfit, although I did like the cape and boots.

Unlike diet pills and weight loss products that usually have lists of side effects that are longer than War and Peace, there are no warnings on the magnetic panties. But I believe there may be a few things you should look out for should you decide to purchase this product. First, there's the chance you may only be able to walk in the direction of true north, which could add a significant amount of time to your daily commute to work should your office be in another direction. You may want to come up with a good excuse for your tardiness that does not start with, "You see, there are magnets in my underwear…"

Then there is the possibility that you will accidentally demagnetize all your credit and debit cards by holding them too close to your body. Now for some of you, this might actually be a good thing, but you need to be forewarned. Always have some cash handy just in case.

Wearing magnetic slimming panties could also really throw your golf game off. Tennis too, if you use a metal racket.

I find it interesting that while scientists have developed magnetic panties, they seem to be lagging behind on magnetic boxer shorts and briefs. Is this because men understand science better than women and therefore realize that there's no way magnets can make them look slimmer? Of course not. We all know the real reason there isn't underwear for men with magnets built in – not only don't they obsess over their hips, stomach, and derriere looking 10 pounds overweight; they only buy underwear once a decade, so there's no real money in it for the manufacturers.

As much as I jest, I will admit that this new scientific breakthrough in underwear did help me. I attached the ad to my refrigerator with a magnet (no, it was not imbedded in a pair of undies). Now every time I go for a snack I have a laugh instead. I feel slimmer already. Thanks magnetic panties!

## Thick Eyelashes and Forests

The worst part of having a cold is and playing hooky from work is being forced to watch hour after hour of daytime TV. Yes, *forced*. When I am too stuffed up and achy to write jokes or head off to teach or talk, I just want to sit on my comfy sofa in my sweats. But when I plop down to rest, my three wiener dogs will immediately take their positions on my lap, which makes doing almost anything but watch TV impossible. You might think I could read, but I have enough experience to know that turning the pages of a book would definitely disturb someone's nap and be met with a glare of wiener dog disappointment. So television it is.

But even the sneeziest of humans can only tolerate a few hours of The Price is Really Loud, The Rich and the Restless, You Might be an Alcoholic (aka, Today with Kathie Lee and Hoda), and Dr. Oz Has Yet Another Disgusting Way to Show You How Your Colon Works. But the shows themselves aren't what saps the life out of you; it's the commercials. In the past sixty minutes, I've learned that I'm too fat, my hair doesn't have enough volume, my eyelashes are "insufficient," my pores are too large, and I may or may not be able to fix all these problems a juicer and or a new cell phone.

I know we humans can be vain and self-centered. After all, I still dye my hair *I Love Lucy Red #17* and try to pass for a 7-year-old. But are there truly men and women who stand in front of a mirror lamenting that their pores are big enough to hide a pirate's treasure? I can't even see my pores without finding my reading glasses first. And why do we all need to have thicker eyelashes—will we need to use them to fly at some point in our evolution?

With so many real problems in the world that are just begging for creative minds to envision solutions, I wonder sometimes why there is so much focus on issues that don't really matter. Perhaps there is a think tank that sits down once a week to prioritize human concerns: "*Let's see, climate change, war, hunger, homelessness, disease, drugs… those are all so depressing. I know, let's try to solve… camel toe!"* Yes, believe it or not, someone has designed and is selling a product for camel toe because apparently thousands of yoga practitioners are suffering.

Fortunately there are scores of people working on important products such as an artificial pancreas for people with diabetes, gravity-powered lights, sight-restoring glasses, and dog strollers. Kudos to them and their creative visions. But if we could just redirect some of the other inventors into focusing on real problems instead of imaginary ones, imagine how much better the world would be.

For example, to the people who created the eyelash thickener… is there any chance if applied to seedlings, we could replenish the rainforests? How do you know if you don't try? Snuggies inventors, listen up. You've made them for lonely single people, for sports lovers, for dogs, and for all I know, chickens. Why not a giant purple Snuggie for the U.S. House of Representatives, so that they all have to move together as a group and perhaps get more things done? We can create a new rule that says no one leaves the House Snuggie until at least three bills are passed.

If you are the brains behind any of the devices that turn water into soda, could you please see if you can make the reverse happen? There are lots of farmers in California, for example, who would love that. For those trying to design clothing to recharge our cell phones, how about clothing that creates enough heat to keep people without homes warm during the winter? And those pore-reducing creams… can we rub a little on to shrink them back down to size?

If you're the folks behind the edible password pill that recently passed FDA inspection and puts a little chip inside our bellies so that our electronic devices recognize us without having to remember our passwords (really, this exists), can you work on a pill that helps us recognize each other without nametags? Millions of baby boomers would benefit from that. I'm not naming names here because…well, I don't remember most of them.

To the inventors of the Booty Pop (an insert to place in the backside of undies to make the, well, booty, uh, pop), please just stop. No good can come of that. On the other hand, if you're in the cell phone app business, could you please create something that opens doors in public buildings so we don't keep spreading colds to each other? I and my dogs would really appreciate it.

**Upgrade This!**

First I got e-mail, then phone calls, then, if you can believe it, snail mail. As much as I enjoy the chase (at least I think I do; it's been awhile), it's not as much fun when the invitations are coming from your internet cable company and are not for a night out on the town but for the "opportunity" to upgrade your modem.

I may be weird (okay, I AM weird), but I'm not the kind of person who needs internet service that is blazingly fast. As long as I can upload videos of cats drinking in the shower within ten seconds, I'm happy. I'm not a gamer or someone who video blogs every day about Twerking or how to make froyo from goats' milk, so the speed I currently have is just fine with me. The truth is, when things go too fast, I get a little freaked out—probably because when I was young my dad decided while on a family outing to see just how fast our car would go (the answer was 125 mph). This was before the invention of seat belts, air bags or blood pressure medication for children. I'm still traumatized whenever someone suggests speeding anything up.

But the cable people (who I envision look like Medusa only with hair made of cables instead of snakes) insisted that sooner or later I would <u>have to</u> upgrade my modem. I made a note on my "To Do Sometime in the Future When I Won't Mind Being Frustrated and Can Do Without Internet for a Day" list. You see, I've upgraded technology before and I know that it's always a bumpy ride.

Yesterday started off well. I got a lot of work done, walked the dogs, and shoveled six wheelbarrows full of dirt. I was feeling on top of the world, so when I noticed "upgrade modem" on my list, I thought, "Okay, I can do that."

It seemed easy. Step 1: Buy new modem so I won't have to pay the monthly rental fee. Check. Step 2: Find old modem and disconnect it. Two hours and five attempts to find a pair of pliers to loosen the cable connection later, check. Step 3: Return old modem to internet company after spending an hour and a half in a waiting room that makes the DMV seem like a bullet train. Check. Step 4: Plug in new modem. I have to admit I thought this would be the worst part; it was not. Check. Step 5: Call internet provider to activate said modem. Checkmate.

My landline is connected to my internet, so I had to call in using my cell phone. Because I rarely use it, it only had one bar (ironically, I later ended up in one bar). I plugged the cell phone and charger into the outlet next to the modem in my guest bedroom to make the call. My phone told me I was "roaming" and would not connect. Apparently breathing and shaking my fish is considered roaming now. I moved into the kitchen and plugged the phone in there. It worked! (I think the dishwasher enhanced its reception.) The call went through, but every time I had to let the customer care agent know which lights on the modem were on or off, I had to put down my cell phone and run into the bedroom. I must have burned off several hundred calories.

After 45 minutes of conversation, my cell phone told me it was too hot. Well, it wasn't the only one. It chose to shut off right in the middle of waiting for customer care agent #3 to come on the line to see if the third time was the charm. I headed across the street to my neighbors' house to borrow their phone. Eventually, it was declared that the modem I had purchased was not compatible with my internet provider. At this point, neither was I.

This morning, after some yoga, a nice long walk with my dogs, and realigning my chakras, I started fresh. A half hour before the office opened, I arrived, only to stand in line with 17 other people who had had the same idea. I decided to rent a modem and started the process over again.

It's a little after noon now and I have internet and home phone service again (hooray!), but my cell phone won't work at all in the house. Apparently, the new modem interferes with cell phone reception. Of course it does. I won't be surprised if my dishwasher melts my flatware or my icemaker makes cotton candy.

As for the speed of the internet, I haven't noticed a change. Perhaps because I haven't logged on yet. I don't need the internet to tell me where the nearest bar is. I was just there last night.

**Hey, Fido, What Are You Watching?**

Whenever I leave the house for more than two hours at a time, I turn on the TV for my dogs. I used to choose Home and Garden TV because like their mother, my dogs enjoy watching paint dry. The problem is that the shows on that channel feature too many people knocking on doors and ringing doorbells, neither of which is conducive to puppy bliss. (I find it extremely odd that none of my dogs has grown up around a doorbell, yet all instinctively know that the sound means someone has come to the house to steal their squeaky toys and drink out of their water dishes.) Home shows also often include the sound of a refrigerator being opened, which automatically causes my pack to rush off their warm spots on the sofa and stand in the kitchen waiting for a free-range, gluten-free, humanely-grown-by-local-farmers-who-love-the-earth-and-all-dogs, miniature organic carrot. Pavlov has nothing on me!

I'm always very careful about what I let my dogs watch on television. One day not too long ago I was watching Ferris Bueller's Day off. There's a scene in that movie in which the principal tries to break into Ferris's house and a Rottweiler growls at him. Less than a second after the growling started, Penny and Watson sprang to their paws, their hackles raised, and began barking as if an asteroid was heading towards earth. Justin, on the other hand, continued his old man nap, snoring and dreaming about even better naps. Clearly a movie channel is too risky business for 2/3 of my pack.

Now when I leave the house I usually tune the TV to Soundscapes, an all-music channel that features new age tunes so relaxing that I can barely make it out the door without snoozing on the welcome mat myself.

But when I discovered DOGTV – a scientifically developed TV network with 24/7 programming designed to stimulate, entertain, relax and alter the behavior of the canine couch potato – of course, I had to check into it. What kind of doggy mom would I be if I didn't?

Unlike television developed for humans (or algae, from the looks of

summer reality programming), DOGTV is based on the science of dogs —
what they hear, see, and think – and features programs from a dog's point of
view. Although true dog's point of view in our house would require that I
put the TV on the floor every time I leave home so that it's at eye level to
my dachshunds. And yes, I have thought about doing that, but I have to
preserve my back so that I can carry the dogs around when they get tired
from rushing to the refrigerator.

As is often the case, the odd quirks in my behavior that have caused
many humans to tilt their heads to one side in confusion when they talk to
me, have proven to have sound science behind them. Research done by
psychologists, animal behavior specialists and the most nerdy of dogs, Labs,
now shows that pooches feel better when the TV is on! Am I a crazy dog
lady or just doggy light years ahead of my time? You decide.

My dogs and I watched three sample DOGTV programs. The first was
Relaxation. The videos of dogs lying around and nodding off to soothing
music immediately sent my crew to dreamland. In part this is because they
had all been sleeping before I insisted they come into my office and watch
the computer (I may have smeared it with peanut butter to encourage their
participation). I started feeling sleepy too. DOGTV may be the cure for my
insomnia.

The Stimulation channel featured dogs playing fetch, swimming,
chasing each other around the yard, and oddly, bats flying. My dogs
continued their naps. They're not very visual creatures. If this channel had
Smell-a-vision, with the aroma of wet poodles and fake bacon made from
soy (they only kind they've ever smelled), they might have actually been
stimulated. The creators of DOGTV say they've enhanced the colors in all
their shows so that dogs can see things better, but clearly their canine focus
group didn't include scent hounds.

The last segment we watched was Exposure, which at first made me
think I'd accidentally turned on doggy porn. The video featured thunder,
doorbells, and sirens – all meant to habituate dogs to daily stimuli. This is a
segment you'd only want to turn on when you're home and can soothe your

pooch with a full body massage.

I do love the idea of DOGTV and might be coerced (or trained) into adding it to our line-up of programs, especially if it's commercial-free. I'm not sure my dogs would watch it, but as much as I hate fireworks and sirens, I'm thinking the Exposure channel might help me and then I could tune into Relaxation and doze off peacefully with my pooches. At least until a doorbell rang.

**What Do Women Want?**

For centuries, men have been asking, "What do women want?" A new book insists that what women really want is more sex. The book is written by a m-a-n. Are you surprised?

Maybe sex is near the top of the list for women who are between the ages of 18 and 45, but if my friends are any barometer (and some are hot enough to be both a barometer and a rain gauge), it's nowhere near the top for the rest of us.

A few years ago a book called What Women Really Want, which was written by two women, made the case that women want power, equality, self-expression, and time to relax. I think that's much closer to the truth, although dog kisses, undergarments that are comfortable and repel bark-o-mulch, and calorie-free key lime pie aren't on the list and they're near the top of mine.

Because I'm curious and love to pester people, I turned on some mystery mood-setting music (The Age of Aquarius) and did a little social media experiment to see if I could discover the truth. I posted the following on my Facebook page: *This is a quick survey. Please only take it if (a) you identify as female, (b) you and I have met in real life, and (c) you don't mind being quoted in one of my columns. The question: What do women really want? You only get one thing. Go!*
I studied epidemiology (that's Latin for "the study of Epi") and statistics in grad school, so I know enough about research to admit that my friends are a biased sample. First of all, they include some silly women who will do anything for laughs. Imagine that—I have silly friends. Who knew? They also tend to cluster between the ages of 40 and 65, probably not the group the guys who wrote the book were talking about. And many of them live in Eugene, OR. (Fill in your favorite Eugene stereotype here; then slap yourself for being so stereotypical. If you don't know anything about Eugene, Google it, now. Go ahead, I'll wait…)

The answers to my very scientific survey ran the gamut from "friends with clean teeth" to "to rule the world!" The one thing that was definitely NOT on the list? Sex. Perhaps my friends are too busy worrying about others' dental hygiene habits or plotting world domination to think carnal thoughts. The most frequently mentioned desire was…insert drum roll here… chocolate. What a surprise—said no woman ever.

Two women mentioned clothing. Melody wanted a bra that fits, while Nancy coveted "a garment that makes my butt look fabulous and has bottomless pockets full of money and chocolate." There were also two votes for world peace, although one was for "whirled peas."

But by far, the majority of my friends wanted empowerment, happiness, contentment, feeling appreciated, respect, and Kung Fu powers. Mary wanted "men to just accept that women are smarter, more compassionate and better leaders, and that if women truly had the power that men currently do, there would be no war. We'd all get along great and our only source of contention would be our fashion decisions." Cheryl summed it up with, "Women want everything including equal pay for equal work, men who like women their own age, strong female pals, and a sense of humor." To quote Leonard from my favorite sitcom The Big Bang theory, "True dat."

While this column was inspired by a recently written book, the central question was asked in a very old book, Canterbury Tales, as friend Judy reminded me. By the way, I had to reread the whole book, which took two weeks and four pairs of reading glasses (I kept losing them in the refrigerator; don't ask). My Middle English is not what it used to be, but I'm that committed to my research. The Wyfe of Bath's Tale tells of a queen who sends a knight on a quest, "*I grante thee lyf, if thou canst tellen me what thing is it that wommen most desyren?*" In other words, the queen offers to spare the knight's life if he can come up with the answer to what women want. The knight asketh every woman he comes upon in his journey (the 14th century version of a FB survey) and is surprised that each woman giveth a different answer. What do you know—women in the 1300s wanted gifts, attention, appreciation, decision-making authority, respect, sexual equality and MORETH.

So there you go. Give us all that and some chocolate that doesn't make us fat and I bet we'll want sex too. Research concluded.

## Bouncy Bouncy

I bought a mini-trampoline this weekend. I was looking for a piece of home fitness equipment that met one specific requirement – it had to fit into a 3-foot square area of my bedroom. All those infomercials that promise muscle toning, core-strengthening, and cardio training neglect to answer the most important question: Will the device fit in your house? Or will you have to remove a major piece of furniture such as the sofa, requiring your guests to perch along the edge of the AbFlexGlideRowArator whenever they come over for margaritas and tofu chili?

Maybe you have a 3600 square foot house with a room designated as "the home gym," but I'm lucky to have a room designated as "the bathroom." The rule around here is nothing new comes in without something old being donated to a local thrift store. This is one reason I never have long-term guests – they worry that I may get up early, hit a few garage sales and come home with a floor lamp that takes up the same amount of space they do. It's a legitimate concern; just ask my half-sister. She was exactly the same size as the wicker clothes hamper I found while she was visiting from California.

When I discovered the mini-tramp (love that word, by the way) at a local sporting goods store and realized it would fit in the bedroom without having to take anything out, I was ecstatic. It didn't hurt that it was only $39 and came in one sleek box. I've had my fill of exercise equipment that arrives in multiple boxes and requires a screwdriver, wrench, hammer, ratchet set, drill press, circular saw, GPS device, latex gloves, and six rolls of duct tape to assemble. I managed to put the mini-trampoline together in less than 15 minutes with just a wrench and the enclosed motivational CD featuring a sexy-sounding man with an Italian accent repeating, "You're a smart and talented woman who can put together this product by yourself. And did I mention how attractive you are?" I got up to my target heart rate just listening to his dulcet tones.

My new "gym" is located right in front of a window so that I can look out at the birds and squirrels while I work out. Perhaps twenty-seven years of living with dogs has affected my brain, but I always feel more energetic when I see creatures darting across the yard. And if I yell "Squirrel!" my dogs also get a workout. It's win-win. The only thing I have to be careful of is not getting overly enthusiastic and hitting my head on my 7-1/2-foot ceiling. I'm pretty sure a concussion doesn't burn extra calories.

Before engaging in my first official bouncing session, I posted the yellow laminated "Trampoline Use Instructions" card in a highly visible place as suggested by the manual. I tacked the card to the closest wall and took a moment to read it over.

- *Do not allow more than one person on the trampoline at a time.* As far as I can tell, the only way that would be possible is if you had a small infant strapped to your chest. So please, if you break into my house with the intent of working out on my mini-trampoline and you happen to have a small infant strapped to your chest, remove said infant prior to getting on the equipment.
- *Use trampoline only with mature, knowledgeable supervision.* Well drat! Where am I going to find someone mature? I have no idea where to even start looking. The most mature person nearby is a neighbor in her eighties, but last week she put Spongebob Squarepants stickers on her bicycle helmet and did her hair like Pippi Longstocking, so she's out.
- *While keeping the head erect, focus eyes on the trampoline toward the perimeter.* I'm sorry, but if my head is erect, I cannot see the trampoline. I know I'm supposed to have a third eye, but not in my ankles. Good thing I have the wiener dogs to keep watch on the perimeter for me… when they're not running for the squirrels.
- *Do not use the trampoline while under the influence of alcohol or drugs.* I'm willing to forgo the booze prior to working out, but what kind of drugs are they talking about? I'm on the estrogen patch and really think using the equipment while experiencing mood swings and hot flashes may be the more dangerous choice. Perhaps I should ask my doctor.

- *Make sure to use the bathroom before using the device.* Okay, it didn't say that, but it should. So I scribbled it on the bottom of the list. I don't want to take any chances.

I'm ready now for my first real workout. Assuming I can find a mature person somewhere.

**To Roof or Not To Roof**

I need a new roof. The one on my house has been there since before the invention of the hammer, which would explain why every time there are heavy winds or more than one butterfly nearby, shingles fly off like parade confetti. The dogs have complained that they are no longer safe in the yard and are tired of playing "duck and cover."

Buying a new roof could dip deeply into my vegan caramel latte and gourmet dog biscuit budget, so I've been procrastinating about taking that plunge. I figured as long as there were no leaks inside the house, I could wait it out. And no, that constant dripping in the garage does NOT count. The garage is OUT THERE.

Lately, however, things aren't looking so good. A neighbor asked whether I was starting a "green roof." Sure, there is some plant life on top of the house, but why bother cleaning off the moss and grass and Doug firs if I'm just going to replace everything in, say, five years? Unfortunately, I discovered a few years ago that a real green roof is not an option for my house, not without beefing up roof rafters as well as the vertical support of the walls. I'm a vegetarian, so that's out.

But I've gotten the message and have started contemplating my choices when it comes to what's overhead.

My major problem is my darned sense of environmental ethics. Whenever I do any home repair, I want to choose the most earth-friendly options. Those are usually also the most expensive, except in the case of caulking around the bathtub. I've found that a nice tube of Tom's toothpaste will do the trick and make everything smell minty fresh for months.

I traipsed off to the most recent home show, investigated the possible roofing choices and quickly decided that I wanted a metal roof. So I wrote down my name and phone number on a card at an exhibitor's booth. A few days later, I had an appointment with the salesman. After looking through a brochure and hundreds of pictures of houses that mine could clearly fit into the bathrooms of, he and I had a conversation that went something like this:

Me: Yes, this is definitely a great product.

Salesman: You won't be sorry you invested in this roof. It's guaranteed for the life of your house or until America's Funniest Videos goes off the air, whichever comes first.

Me: Okay, but before making any decision, I have to know the estimated cost. That's just the kind of woman I am.

Salesman: I've done the walk-around, taken some measurements, and stepped in some dog poo, which will cost you extra, by the way. Your price, if you sign the contract before I leave the house, would be...

At this point, he pulled out a piece of paper and wrote a number on it. He turned it over and slid it towards me. My heart a-flutter, I flipped the paper and read the amount: $30,000.17!

Three minutes, one round of CPR, and a glass of juice later, I finally came to on the floor. The dogs had encircled me and Penny was going through my pockets looking for cookies.

Me: $30,000?

I tried no to shriek, but I failed.

Salesman: And 17 cents. For the dog poo.

Me: But I only paid $82,000 for the house to begin with.

Salesman: I understand that it seems like a lot of money...

Me: No. It doesn't seem like a lot of money; it IS a lot of money. I could purchase 731 shares of Facebook for that amount. I could buy an RV and outfit it with special ramps and doggy doors for the dachshunds and we could travel the country in search of fire hydrants until the price of gas reaches $6 a gallon. I could finally get my teeth cleaned.

Salesman: But you would never EVER have to replace the roof again.

Me:  That may be true, but I already may have to replace my heart and most of my hair, just from having read the estimate. Imagine what writing the checks would do to me.

He left sadly disappointed. I attempted to meditate to reduce my blood pressure.

Since then I've gotten an estimate for roofing tiles made from recycled rubber tires ($23,000) and 25 rolls of heavy-duty aluminum foil ($100, but I'd have to get up on the roof to do the job myself and I'm afraid of the snakes that are probably hiding in the grass).

Meanwhile, the roof garden continues to grow and I'm contemplating how many brownies it would take to entice my neighbor to get up there and mow. That I could probably afford.

## It's My Party, Where's My Pony?

This is my birthday month. I'll be 36. Well, I will be if I calculate my age in base 17, which I do. That's right, being a math geek pays off big as you get older! If you want, I can calculate your age for you as well. Just let me find my old slide rule.

Many other "36"-year-olds want to forget they even have a birthday. They prefer to roll up in the fetal position in a closet and whimper softly as they contemplate their own mortality. That does NOT sound like the kind of party I want to be invited to. I wouldn't even know what to wear or what kind of gift to bring.

For my birthday, I want a cake. I want ice cream. I want a pony. I've been waiting "36" years for a pony, so it's about time she shows up on my front stoop with a red bow woven through her mane. I'll name her Peony and let her graze on the flowers in my back yard. And yes, I will let her sleep in my bed with the dogs and me. I hope she doesn't kick.

At my party, I want singing and laughter. Enough with the whining about things that used to be cool that are now sweaty and things that used to be located properly on the body that are now significantly further south, say in Brazil. I figure my boobs are happier partying in Rio de Janeiro than they were perched squarely on the middle of my torso. As long as no one makes them wear a bikini.

It's hard to understand why so many of my friends turn into whiners as they get older. Our bodies have always changed. When I was two I could fit both feet in my mouth. Now I can only get one in there and only metaphorically. At four, did I complain that I was getting old? I'm fairly certain I was too busy having fun to look back. Now that I'm "36," why should I spend all my time comparing who I am to who I used to be. That woman, as fond of her as I me, is now only a figment of my imagination.

The truth is, I wouldn't trade places with my twenty-something self for all the money in the world. All the chocolate… maybe. I teach 20-

somethings and I don't want their problems, no ma'am! I'm much happier watching my goatee grow in than I was worrying about whether so-and-so liked me or if I had missed my Econ midterm.

So let's all just party like we're 36 and stop looking back. The view from here is pretty damned good. And wait, do I smell pony?

## ARF Parenting

You may be wondering whether you're a good dog parent. If you are not scratching a belly with one hand while doling out cookies with the other, all while reading this column, the answer is "Not yet, but you CAN be!" On the other hand, if you wake up every morning with an aching back because you sleep like a circus contortionist in order to provide sufficient space for a hound or five, you can rest easy... or not... when it comes to doing a good job raising your four-legged children.

After 30 human years as mom to canines small and smaller, I can honestly say that I am an expert in what some consider "spoiling" but I know is just good dog parenting. There are plenty of books out there for moms and dads of companion children, but not many for canines. If you hear the pitter-patter of two-footed creatures running around the house, you can choose to be an *attachment parent* (I believe Velcro is involved), *a Tiger mother* (Rawr!) or, the latest sensation, *a CTFD parent* (Calm the Fudge\* Down). (\*Semantics have been changed to protect the innocent.)

For those of you with questions about parenting kids who bark instead of mumble, and who don't roll their eyes but stare deeply into yours as if trying some kind of Vulcan mind-meld technique to get you to give them extra treats, there are no official parenting techniques, so I have invented one. I call it ARF or *Always Roll-over for Fido*. I'll use the ARF technique to answer some of your important questions.

Q: My dog just won't quit barking. Should I comfort her or just let her bark herself to sleep?

A: Barking is a sign that something is off-kilter in the doggone universe. Your hound may be wet, dry, hungry, full, inside, outside, in need of a stuffed animal, buried by too many stuffed animals, wondering whether Einstein was right about parallel lines meeting somewhere in the cosmos...Your job as an ARF parent is to figure out the source of the problem and fix it. Then the barking will stop…until something else comes up.

Q: The human members of the family haven't been to the dentist in ages, but I take my dog to get his teeth cleaned every year. I feel guilty about that. What should I do?

A: I suggest therapy. Let's face it, the rest of the family can brush, floss, and gargle, but your pooch relies on you to keep his teeth clean. Brush them every night and keep up the professional cleanings. Doggy breath might make it less likely that you'll smooch the pooch when he does something wonderful, such as wake up from a nap.

Q:  I have a poodle named Steve and he insists on dressing in all the latest designer doggy duds. How do I say no?

A:  That's not Steve (really, Steve?) talking, it's the voices in your head. Dogs prefer to be naked. If you must shop for fancy clothes, don't blame the hound.

Q: My dog keeps trying to get on the furniture? What should I do?

A: Clearly, you've made it too difficult for her to get up on the sofa or bed. Your best bet is to build a series of ramps. If you have no skills, call a handyman with experience in crafting canine furnishings because you need someone who can hammer without breaking into fits of laughter.

Q: Since our last family photo, we've gotten a new dog. Can we just Photoshop him into the picture?

A: Unless you would also cut and paste a photo of a new human baby into a family portrait, no! Make an appointment with an expensive photographer now for the whole family. And apologize to your hound for even thinking such a thing.

Q: If my dog gets a minor injury, how do I know when to visit the vet?

A: Your best bet in ARF parenting is to have married a vet, but if you didn't have that foresight, always err in favor of checking things out. Sure eventually you'll pay for at least two new vehicles and perhaps a helicopter for the doggy doctor, but it's worth it for the peace of mind. After the appointment, you may also need to visit a doggy physical therapist. My dachshund Watson visited a doggy physical therapist (no, the therapist was not canine) this past summer, where he walked on an underwater treadmill. We're still waiting to see whether he'll be offered a contract to represent Nike or Reebok.

Q: One of my dogs is getting older and can't walk as fast as the others. Should I leave him home while we go on our outings?

A: Really? Would you leave grandma home while everyone else goes to Disneyland? Okay, forget that… The answer is still, "No." This is what doggy strollers are for. If you can't afford one because you're tapped out from the physical therapy and teeth cleaning, a stroller built for humans can be adapted for small to medium-sized dogs. If your senior dog is a Great Dane or a Newfie, a large garden wagon outfitted with comfy cushions is your best choice. So what if people point and stare.

There you are—all the basics for ARF parenting. Now go, rub some bellies!

**Teetering on the Brink**

This is an intervention. The people who love you are concerned about what you are doing to yourself. We feel you may have an addiction… to cute shoes with high heels.

It started off so innocently, when you were playing dress-up and slipped on mom's Mary Janes with the 1" heel in the third grade. We admit it was cute hearing you clip-clop across the hardwood floors, like a miniature horse wearing pearls and a Sunday hat. If only we had known then what we know now.

In retrospect, those Mary Janes were a gateway drug. By freshman year of high school you had graduated to pumps with a 2" heel. We tried to stop you. We offered you other options—sandals, sneakers, flip-flops… but you turned us down cold. We even showed you pictures of girls your age rocking Uggs with mini-dresses, but you called us "squares" and did your best to stomp out of the house without twisting an ankle.

We were relieved when two years later you went through your Goth phase and traded in your heels for a pair of lace-up combat boots. Even though your black-lip-sticked mouth was in a perpetual frown, we knew that your feet at least were happy and that made us happy too. But then college came and you succumbed to peer pressure and got sucked right back into the hard and heartless world of high heels.

Never in our wildest dreams did we imagine you would fall this far. We kept waiting for your willpower and self-control to kick in. Now we know we were foolish to procrastinate this long. Had we stepped up earlier, perhaps we could have saved you from the 6" heels of death you now consider to be part of your everyday wardrobe. We shudder when we see you wobble across the driveway, your ankles looking as if they could snap at any moment. When we're in the passenger seat and you are driving, we're concerned for our own lives, knowing full well there is no way you can properly brake with your foot at a 75 degree angle to the floor. The dog is scared to come anywhere near you for fear he'll be gored.

Don't get us wrong. We understand how powerful the pull of high heels can be. There are so many tempting choices—the reds, the whites, the leopard print with pink zippers on the sides. And the pushers are everywhere—in malls, online, and operating fly-by-night shoe operations from the trunks of their cars. They don't care about you; they just want to keep you hooked.

We know that high heels can make you look taller and lift the junk in your trunk up higher than natural. We know that when you're wearing them you turn heads at the office and on the streets, especially on the streets. In fact, exotic dancers and women who work the streets have been the primary customer of the treacherous footwear your closet it filled with. Oh, and drag queens. Why do you think they have those strappy 6" platform sandals in your size? Don't tell us men haven't offered you single dollar bills as you wait for the bus. Don't tell us you haven't been toying with the idea of taking a stripper-cise class. We know you have. We can see it in your eyes.

We're okay with people confusing you for something you're not because we know who you are inside. But we're worried about the physical repercussions your "habit" may cause now and in the future—the foot pain, the bunions, the hip trouble, the inability to walk in slippers, the fear of sloped streets, the paranoia that someone will walk up behind you and shove you off your stilts, uh, shoes.

This, dear friend, is why we have gathered today. We are the sisterhood of the comfortable shoe and we beg you to join us. Please recant your unhealthy nasty habit and join us in our Birkenstocks and Danskos and Crocs for the good life you were meant to live.

If you can't make the change on your own, we are here for you. We will meet you every week for a foot massage and a reminder that we love you short, flat-footed, and not limping home at the end of the day. We promise you'll be happier. And so will the dog.

## I'm No Cougar

I was innocently watching something on TV the other night when an ad for a dating site popped up. It was called OlderWomenWithoutBoundaries.com or something like that. Naturally, I had to run to the computer to check it out -- not because I am one (a cougar), mind you, but because I needed good laugh.

I found there are actually several dating sites for cougars (none for pumas, panthers or housecats, however). I logged onto CougarLife.com because it said it was #1 in cougar dating; it was rated four claws. Across the top of the home page was a picture of a blond woman reclining on the floor, wearing a robe and panties. I knew I had found the right site, not because of her outfit, but because as a woman over a certain age, I know that reclining is the best position to be photographed in. It relieves the pull of gravity on breasts, derriere, and jowls. It's the poor woman's plastic surgery. Those who can afford surgery never lie down. They can't. Everything is too tight.

According to CougarLife.com, a cougar is a woman in her PRIME (Prefers Raunchy and Immature Men Exclusively). She must also be independent, sexy and wildly successful. Apparently, I couldn't be a cougar even if I wanted. I've got the independent part down and with a day at the spa, the right lighting, and a myopic partner, can fake the sexy, but no one would ever mistake me for wildly successful. I don't even know the difference between bears and bulls, except at the zoo. The IRS has made reviewing my pitiful income tax returns into a drinking game. "Okay, we do a shot every time she puts a decimal in the wrong place!"

But, back when I was 32, I met a guy while out dancing who was right out of college. I wasn't "on the prowl," as cougars are known to be. I just enjoy dancing and the only men who could keep up with me at the time were in their 20s. I was both a marathon runner and an aerobics teacher and had the stamina of a hummingbird. Today I have the stamina of a well-fed penguin.

Had there been such a term at the time, I guess I qualified as a cougar. I was even much more wildly successful, if by successful you mean "earning enough money to go out dancing twice a week." However, I made the ultimate cougar mistake. After only a few months of dating, I married the "cub" as they're known in cougarese. If this happened today, I would have been kicked out of the den because everyone knows that if you're closer in age to his mother than to him, things are going to get weird quickly. Which is why I'm single again... but still not a cougar.

## It Ain't Easy Being Green

I start off each new year resolving to become a more environmentally responsible citizen of the planet. Earth, to be specific.

In other parts of the country, my solar panels and organic garden might be considered signs of a truly committed conservationist, but in Oregon there are people so green they make Al Gore look like a sustainability drop-out. Keeping up with the Jones' is difficult when they ride their bikes to work, bathe in mud puddles, and generate their own electricity by rubbing hemp balloons on their fair-trade sisal rugs.

But I do try. Three years ago, I committed to remembering to actually USE the canvas bags I had purchased back in the 90s. At first this was difficult because I had gotten accustomed to having my bags accompany me to the store, but leaving them behind in the car as if they were not welcome inside. One day I tossed them all in the laundry with the hopes that once they were clean and presentable, I'd be more likely to let them do the job they were meant to do. My plan worked, but not for the reason you might think. The first time I handed the bags over to a grocery cashier, he stopped cold. Clearing his throat, he whispered, "I think you left some, uh, laundry in this bag." Then he handed me a pair of my panties. To this day, I double-check my bags for stray lingerie, but I DO remember to bring them with me. Apparently my memory runs on heavy doses of public humiliation.

The next year I resolved to use my dryer only for blankets and sheets. For the most part, I've managed to keep this resolution. In the spring and summer, I line dry everything outside in the sun. The other ten months of the year, I hang everything from a rack. And yes, I am damp and chilly most of the time, but that disadvantage is more than balanced out by the conversational value of airing out my "stuff" in the living room. The look on the UPS guy's face when he shows up at my front door on laundry day is priceless.

Last year's resolution was to stop using personal care products and make-up with petroleum-based products and toxic chemicals. This has been a tough one, but I haven't yet taken to rubbing dirt on my face in lieu of foundation, although it is a lot cheaper than those mineral make-ups they sell on infomercials. If only compost came in my skin shade, which according to a recent color consultation, is known as "Paste." Occasionally I do miss people telling me, "Mmmm, you smell nice!" when they catch a whiff of my soap or shampoo. These days I have to settle for "What's that, uh, earthy smell?" But hey, bark-o-mulch makes an excellent exfoliant.

Now I'm trying to decide on the next step of my journey to becoming a better steward of this little piece of the earth. There are so many possibilities and I'm aware of all of them because I watch a lot of "green" TV shows such as Living With Ed Without Suffocating Him With a Down-Alternative Pillow While He Sleeps. And yes, I realize that watching television is a wasteful activity, but I can't kill my TV because five years ago I resolved to be non-violent.

Did you know there are people who have committed to eat only things that are grown within 100 miles of their towns? I thought about making this my resolution until I realized I'd have to give up coffee AND chocolate. I think I'd have to move to South America first and that's a l-o-n-g walk. I can't fly there because that wouldn't be good for the planet. Although on the plus side, if I did move, my laundry would be a lot drier

Finally, after mulling over my options, I hit on the perfect idea. Mother Earth and I have something in common these days – we're both hot-flashing. And although many people joke about menopausal women causing the planet to heat up, no one's done anything about it. I plan to find someone who can hook me up to a battery so I can produce my own energy. It's the obvious choice. Maybe I could produce enough power to use my electric toothbrush without feeling guilty.

That's my plan, but I hope I've inspired you to try your own green resolutions too. Because as we all know, hell hath no fury like a woman scorched.

## Summer is Going Swimmingly

I love summer in Oregon for many reasons, but somewhere near the top of the list is the fact that there's no real pressure to wear a bathing suit. Hailing originally from the south, I can't tell you how much better I feel each spring not hearing women utter that phrase that always sends shivers up my pasty spine, "I have to get in shape for swimsuit season."

This is not to say that I don't own a swimsuit; I do. It's the official Oregon swimsuit though – flannel with long sleeves, a hood, and detachable hip waders. I even paid extra for the optional sand goggles. Believe me, they're worth it.

A friend of mine from Texas visited me last summer. She'd never been to our fair state and wanted to see the famous Oregon coast, so I drove her to Florence. After about five minutes of standing in the fog with the wind whipping by, she shouted, "It's too cold! It's too windy! Where are all the tan people?""

We retreated to the car, where she cranked up the heater and slapped her thighs to jumpstart her blood flow.

"You're looking at this all wrong," I told her. "People don't come to the Oregon coast to play beach volleyball or put the finishing touches on their tan. We come for the free exfoliation." I showed her my smooth skin. "This would cost thousands of dollars if I had to go to a dermatologist."

I laughed. Perhaps she was laughing too, but her teeth were chattering so hard that it was hard to tell.

Unlike many of my fair-weather friends, I love the cool, often damp and windy weather along our beaches. As a natural redhead – that IS what it says on the box – I'm supposed to avoid too much exposure to the sun. I can't tell you how nice it is to be able to go outside without having to don a hat the size of golf umbrella and smearing SPF 400 on my nose and shoulders. I'm much more comfortable in a windbreaker and ski cap and here I fit right in with the rest of the beach-goers.

I also like the fact that people on Oregon beaches are always on the move. Unlike California, Florida, or Texas, where almost everyone lies around on towels reading trashy novels, coastal folk here search for sand dollars at a 7 mph clip or chase their dogs as their dogs chase the seagulls. (If those dogs happen to be named *Steve* and *Emily* while their owners go by *Rainforest* and *Starshine*, you can be fairly certain they're not out-of-state visitors, by the way). Before I moved to Oregon fifteen years ago, I heard that the people in this state were an active lot. What I didn't know was that this is primarily because you could catch pneumonia if you stand still for too long. Or disappear for hours into a bank of fog.

Visitors may be surprised that they have to dress warmly and serpentine down the beach, but it's just part of what makes our summers unique. Plus, if you don't have to devote half your weekend to making sure your tan lines are even, you have so much more time to browse through art galleries and dine at all the wonderful restaurants nearby.

But when it comes down to the real truth, not having to try on last year's bathing suit only to find that it no longer fits and I'll have to face the horror of shopping for a new one that covers up my "problem areas" and accentuates my assets (primarily my teeth and gums), is the true reason I love our coastal climate. Sure they have miracle suits now that promise to make five pounds of your tummy disappear, but I remember Newton's Third Law, which states that for every action there is an equal and opposite reaction. This means that if five pounds of my stomach disappears, it's going to reappear somewhere else. I don't know about you, but the idea of strolling along a beach and finding those extra five pounds hanging between my shoulder blades or stacked up under my chin just gives me the willies.

I'm just happy as an Oregon clam with our summer weather on the coast. No one ever says "I have to get in shape for the rainy season," and that suits me just fine.

## Elementary, My Dear Watson

Watson the Dachshund's becoming the latest member of the Jasheway family all started because of a dachshund group I belong to that has been around since before Facebook (yes, I realize those were the dark ages of the internet, but there are some of us who remember communicating via something called e-mail). One day in late December 2011, I noticed a group e-mail in my box from a woman named Martha who was looking for a home for a large wiener dog whose human mom had passed away. Before engaging my brain (or asking permission from the two heads of my household, Justin and Penny, both wiener dogs themselves), I sent a return message saying I'd consider adding him to my family.

Three hours later, Martha and Watson are sitting in my living room, with a checklist to see if this might be the place he could call home from now on. Martha is Watson's human sister and she had tried to make him part of her family, but realized that he was unhappy being cooped up in her tiny apartment during her long hours at work. She wanted someone who would neglect other parts of life—things such as bathing and leaving the house – to make sure Watson had the attention he needed.

She glanced around the room at the ramps up to the sofa and window seat, the two dog beds, five dog blankets, fourteen stuffed animals, and sectional sofa upon which Justin and Penny held court. They had already sniffed both human and canine guest and seemed assured that neither was a burglar or had smuggled in any type of meat product.

"This looks like the place, Watson," Martha said. "Don't you think?"

I'm not sure he heard her, as he clomped down the hallway to see what fun things he might dig up. I say "clomped" because Watson is a 23-lb. dachshund with paws more befitting a Clydesdale horse.

Martha and I followed him for the rest of the tour of the house. I showed them the ramp up to the king-sized bed. The dog patio. The collection of dog sweaters, t-shirts, and party outfits.

"I can see how much you love your dogs," she said, tears beginning to stream down her face.

"And I can see how much you love Watson, too." We both cried. "He knows you're doing this for him," I reassured her.

"I hope so."

An hour or so later she left. Watson paced by the window and barked a few times, with a bark that is also somehow more befitting of a Clydesdale or perhaps a Sasquatch. When he barks his whole long dog body elevates above the floor. It didn't take long however for him to sense that this was now his place and we were his new family. He immediately claimed one of the dog beds as his, grabbed two stuffed animals in his mouth at a time, and snuggled under a blanket.

Because ours is an open adoption, I regularly send Martha photos and updates at Watson's escapades—how he stole all my strawberries and tomatoes this summer, how he learned to open the closet of dead stuffed animals, how he has joined Justin in the 4 a.m. march of the wiener dogs across my stomach so that I have no choice but to get up and feed everyone breakfast.

Every time I look at pictures of other dogs in need of homes, at least one of mine will sit at my feet to remind me that I am only one e-mail or telephone call away from that first step on the path of becoming a crazy dog lady.

## Yes, I'm Older than You and I'm Okay with That

Who knew when I got my bachelor's degree in political science in the last millennium that I'd end up with college students calling me "Professor"? Officially I'm an instructor but if students want to call me "professor" or even "goddess," I am okay with that.

I like teaching college students. They're full of energy and big ideas and on days when they're not coughing and sneezing directly on me, being around them is energizing. I walk faster, I think more deeply about life, and I am much more aware of everything going on around me at all times because if I am complacent for even a few seconds, someone on a skateboard will plow me down.

Keeping company with people much younger than I am does, however, remind me that I am old. In their eyes, I am ancient. As we all know, "ancient" is defined as "whatever age you are + 20 years." It really doesn't matter if I dye my hair green, quote Drake and Adele (ask your kids), or wear a t-shirt emblazoned with YOLO (you only live once), I'm not fooling anyone. In an effort to sound hip, I once said to a student, "Like totally awesome, dude," to which he shook his head and stared above me as if I was wearing bell bottoms and listening to disco tunes.

The fact is, we come from different generations. Mine didn't trust anyone over 30, so why should theirs? But now that I'm on the other side of the generational fence (way on the other side), I'm not embarrassed by the fact that they think people my age are "lame." I thought the same thing about my own professors. I had a 50-something male calculus professor who wore stretch denim jeans to class every day. We all thought that was so stupid. He's probably laughing all the way to the bank today, having invented the fabric that every middle aged woman adores.

Why must we pretend to be up-to-date and with-it? By the way, I'm fairly certain "with-it" is not a with-it word. Can't we be happy knowing we grew up in another time? A time when, in my case, students learned to do math in their heads. Most students today just ask their cell phones to figure out how much to tip or how much interest has accrued on their student loans. When Siri or whoever relays the information back to them, they think it's some kind of magic, like sawing a professor in half. Abracadabra! I'm okay with that.

I'm proud that when I was in college, I got to walk around listening to the birds and the protestors because my ears were free of headphones. Portable music devices such as the Walkman wouldn't show up until 1980 and it was hard to get to class with an 8-track tape deck duct-taped to your back (and even harder to avoid tripping over the 500-foot extension cord.) These days, it appears that ear buds have become part of human anatomy. If I see anyone under 20 with nothing in his ears, I wonder if he had a horrible accident that rendered him permanently disconnected from his iPod. We're technologically different. I'm okay with that.

When I went to college at the University of Texas when dirt was being discovered, we sat in the same hard wooden chairs most classrooms still use today (it's more difficult to sleep deeply when your rear end and spine are screaming out in agony). We were occasionally distracted by daydreams about the weekend or the big debate tournament (yes, I was a nerd), but we didn't have cell phones and tablet devices constantly clamoring for our attention. That meant our parents couldn't check up on us 24/7. And that was like totally amazing, dude! We couldn't tweet our friends or give our professor a lousy review on YELP because she was giving too much homework. Times have changed. I'm okay with that.

We typed our papers on typewriters and used Liquid Paper to blot out spelling and grammatical errors. I sometimes arrived in class a little high from Liquid Paper fumes, but every generation has that problem, right? When we did research, we HAD to go to the library and use the *card catalog* to find *books* on the subject. There was no Internet, no Google search, no Wikipedia to tell us lies about math, science, and history. What took us hours can be had in a few seconds online today. I'm okay with that. Lastly, and this may be the weirdest difference of all, I don't remember drinking water. We certainly didn't carry around bottles of water everywhere we went. There were water fountains and if we got thirsty, we drank out of them. Apparently, mine was a generation of camels. In week 7 of my largest class, there were 38 water bottles in the lost and found behind the podium. They're a thirsty crew, this group. I'm okay with that too.

Regardless of labels – greatest generation, boomers, slackers, millenials – we all have our own unique history and we should honor and celebrate it. In fact, I think I'll wear my bell-bottoms and dig out my old Sony Walkman to wear to class today. The students will think I'm old and lame. I'm okay with that.

## Home Show, Sweet Home Show

I love home shows! The design ideas, the free goodies, the workshops with names so appealing they cause you to lose all sense of perspective about your own home… At a recent event, I attended a workshop called "You Too Can Have a Spa Bath at Home." The contractors showed slides of walk-in showers with enough room for the entire Angelina Jolie-Brad Pitt family. The shower had a rain wall and eight separate wall-mounted showerheads. It was only as I picked up a brochure on my way out that I remembered that my entire bathroom barely has enough room for me and one dachshund (as with all moms, I never get to go to the bathroom alone). What was I thinking?

But who can resist seminars with titles such as Adorable Alpacas! (exclamation mark included) and Chickens Over the Aisle? I went to those too, thinking that perhaps the wiener dogs would let me keep alpacas and chickens in the back yard if I gave them more cookies. So far, I'm fulfilling my need for suburban farming by chicken-sitting for my neighbors. There are eight egg-laying girls across the street and whenever I arrive, they greet me with love and affection, as though I'm a long-lost aunt. They may actually just come rushing at me because they know I'm going to toss extra chicken scratch their way, but I can still feel the love.

Regularly attending home shows tends to make me more critical of my own abode and, as a result, I often want to jump on the remodeling bandwagon. I bought the house I'm in twenty-years ago while on vacation. In fact, I signed the paperwork two hours before having to catch a plane back to Texas. Talk about a vacation souvenir.

But I'm still here and that's something. However, so far I have (and by "I have," I mean "my lovely contractor Mark Richardson and a team of other handy people have") added two new windows, a bay window for the dogs and three skylights to make the long gray winter days more visible from the inside; replaced all the flooring; lost a bedroom (well, I know where it is… it's in my "master suite" now); updated the bathroom from the oak outhouse style that left splinters well, you know where; had the kitchen remodeled with my then-controversial-now-quite-trendy turquoise cabinets, yellow backsplash tile, and periwinkle countertops; replaced the back patio because I was tired of weeding between the cracks; added a pond with four fabulous koi, Picasso, Goldie, Moby, and Spot; installed solar water panels and heater; and painted every room in the house at least six times. Just to be clear, I did the painting myself. This is not boasting so much as taking responsibility for the drips and unevenness around the ceilings and corners.

Now that I think about it, I may have a psychological problem. Is there such thing as HDD – Home Decorating Disorder?

The one thing in my house that hasn't changed is the original 1965 turquoise GE stove in the kitchen. It doesn't work well. It has push-buttons in the front, so every time you lean up against them (which is often as the kitchen is only slightly larger than the bathroom), the burners light up. This is not a stove you want to leave a paper bag on, even for a few seconds. Every time I intentionally turn a burner on, the smell of 48 years of cooking scares my dog, Penny. Most of the time instead of using the oven, I rely on a portable convection oven than I store in the turquoise stove. But turquoise is such a pretty color for a stove. In fact the entire color scheme in my house was chosen as an accent to it. Not to mention that while at a home show recently I discovered that in order to replace a 27" stove, which mine is, I'd have to shell out about $3,000. And that doesn't include having it painted turquoise.

My continual home improvement isn't rooted in trying to keep up with the Joneses, or in my case, the Jacobsons, Klohns, and Readys. It's just that I spend a lot of time at home because the dachshunds only occasionally let me leave the house. If they see me putting on make-up, they swarm around the bathroom door in an attempt to trip me on the way out. So the money other people would spend on restaurants, bars, fancy cars, vacations, and alpacas, I spend feathering our nest (but only with feathers of free-range, organic, chicken nieces from across the street).

Besides, making all these improvements to a house that is almost as old as I am keeps me from focusing on my own aging. When it comes down to choosing between Botox and tiling the fireplace, I'm going with the tiles every time. I can always pull my hair into tight pigtails, but the fireplace doesn't have that option.

**New Technology Definitions**

Trexting – Tripping while texting

Unpinteresting – Something not as appealing as it seemed on Pinterest

Instagrammy – Grandmothers who keep sending photos of their vacations to their grandkids

Lordipediacs – Those who believe everything written in their good book, Wikipedia

Twit – Anyone who spends hours trying to put his or her feelings into 140 characters or   less

Nownsense – The irrational belief that all texts must be answered NOW!

GPStupid – Anyone willing to drive off a cliff because their GPS device tells them too; see also Map Questers

Pseudoposters – Those who post glowing comments on their own websites using   pseudonyms

Trend-bender – Someone who seeks out activities and information that aren't trending

Shelfies – People who are bad at taking selfies and usually end up with pictures of the furniture behind them

**Spoiler Alert**


A few nights ago, I decided it was time for the dogs to have a nice evening walk. Why not take advantage of the longer days to enjoy the sights and sounds (and smells) of the neighborhood at night, I thought.

However, it being still warm outside and I being the mother of canines who firmly believe that when the temperature exceeds 72 degrees, they should not have to leave the comfort of the sofa (unless it is to run outside and eat birdseed in the yard), I decided we would utilize the Wiener Wagon.

Those of you who follow my exploits already know that I have a baby stroller retrofitted for tired dachshunds. But the stroller will only hold two pooches (unless I perch Penny on the canopy on top, which I would never do, except that once when she refused to walk if both brothers got to ride). So, it makes sense that I recently purchased a foldable canvas wagon that will easily accommodate three, if not four, wiener dogs. (If anyone at the Humane Society is reading this, please do not let me adopt another dachshund! I rely on you to keep my addiction in check.)

So off we went, ambling around the neighborhood. Well, I ambled. The dogs on the other hand, enjoyed the evening air and the view without having to exert any effort whatsoever. Might I add here that they totally love not doing any work on a walk. As for me, I'm not sure pulling 67 pounds of dogs plus whatever the wagon weighs can officially be called "ambling." But it most definitely wasn't speed-walking.

As I waved to neighbors who either think I'm a good dog mom or a woman who has gone off her rocker (or both), I decided it's time once again to play one of my favorite games – Is Your Dog Spoiled Enough? And since playing alone isn't any fun, you're invited. Ready?

Answer yes or no to each of the following questions:

1.  Let's start with transportation. Not counting your car, do you have two or more wheeled forms of transportation for your canine? If you

occasionally carry him in a Baby Snuggie or tuck him in your shirt, go ahead and select "yes."

2.  When walking your dog on a sunny day, do you position your body between your hound and the sun's rays and walk at just the right speed to make sure she always has shade?

3.  On a walk, do you walk at the speed of dog (whether that is lightning-fast greyhound or stop- and-smell-the-everything Basset Hound) even if it threatens to send you to the hospital with a heart attack or you miss your next three meetings?

4.  Now on to health and well-being. Do you have a baby guard on your bed (of course your dog sleeps in your bed!) to prevent poochie from rolling over in his sleep and falling on the floor?

5.  Does your dog take more vitamins and supplements than you do, including one for mental clarity?

6.  Rather than tossing your dog a treat, do you either place it directly in her mouth or chew it into small bites beforehand?

7. Has your canine seen two or more of the following specialists: acupuncturist, naturopath, chiropractor, massage therapist, dog psychologist, orthodontist, or Chinese herbalist?

8.  Does he have his own yoga mat and understand the words "downward dog," "warrior pose" and "Namaste"?

9.  Our last set of questions are about your canine's social life. Does your dog have his own Facebook or Pinterest page?

10.  Have you ever had a human soiree at your home in which the humans stayed in the yard or garage while the dog(s) remained in the air conditioned/heated house?

11.  When you do allow humans in the house, have you ever asked them nicely to sit on the floor so as not to disturb the sleeping canine(s) on the sofa?

12.  When sending out invitations for your pooch's birthday bash, do you consider which font she would prefer?

      Okay, the rest is easy. Count the number of "yes" answers you chose. If it is six or fewer, you definitely need lessons in how to appropriately spoil a hound. If you had 7-10 yes answers, you're good, but not good enough. Look deeply into your dog's eyes and ask yourself if you shouldn't try harder. Revisit those spoiling techniques you have not yet adopted or make up some of your own so that you don't bring your dog shame on his or her social media page, aka, fire hydrant.
      My score, by the way, was 11. I'll let you guess which question I answered "No" to. But know that I'll start working on correcting my shortcoming as soon as I get back from wheeling the Wiener Wagon to the doggy naturopath.

### Can You Hear Me Now?

I recently joined a gym in order to get back in shape. "Get back in shape" is an odd phrase, don't you think? Any shape you're in is *a shape*— even if you're trapezoidal. Really, shouldn't we say, "I want to get into a shape that is less like a curvilinear triangle" (or whatever geometric object you happen to resemble)?

But I digress... My re-dedication to working out was inspired when I noticed an extra ring around my midsection, as though someone had snuck in during the night and Gorilla Glued a squishy hula hoop to my waist. Mind you, I've never been small enough to fit into a designer dress (because those are all created for imaginary women who maintain their birth weight through their 20s), nor am I obsessed with my body and what it looks like (except for that time I took an Advil PM because I couldn't sleep and dreamed I was a starfish). I have accepted the personalized continental drift that comes with aging, with certain landmasses moving overnight. I've even made peace with the fact that my once concave stomach now features a built-in airbag so I don't bruise as easily when I run into things.

An extra ring of fat around my waist, however, is something I can change. So off I headed to the nearest local gym, plunked down my debit card, and signed up for a month. My membership came with an hour-long free personal trainer consultation. A young man named Spencer, who was 6'7" and had the body fat of the statue of David, asked me a series of questions about my exercise history and fitness goals.

Spencer: What brings you to the gym?

Me: Well, to be honest, a 50% off coupon and a little extra belly fat. Oh, and I've started hot flashing again so I thought I might as well join others who are spending their days sweaty and miserable.

Spencer averted his eyes. I've discovered that young men tend to be very shy when the topic turns to things menopausal. After a few seconds, he mustered up the strength to continue the interview.

> Spencer: So, what are your fitness goals?
>
> Me: I'd like to lose a few points, but mostly gain some core strength and improve my balance.
>
> Spencer: That's great. So many people come in with unreasonable goals like looking like Leighton Meester.

I did not let on that I have no idea who Leighton Meester is. I simply nodded in agreement. I don't want to have unreasonable goals such as believing a few minutes on a treadmill will turn me into a woman less than half my age (I Googled her when I got home).

> Spencer: Okay, this is the question I hate to ask, but I have to... how old are you?
>
> Me: 57.

Spencer looked honestly shocked.

> Spencer: No way! You look so much younger. How do you do it?
>
> Me: Mostly avoiding the sun.

Spencer stared at his well-tanned biceps and frowned.

> Spencer: I guess I'm out of luck then.
>
> Me: Well, there are also the dog kisses.

He looked at me quizzically. I decided not to share my belief that dog saliva contains anti-aging properties.

Spencer:  What kinds of exercise do you do regularly?

Me: Wiener dog walking and extreme gardening.

Spencer:  Extreme gardening? What's that?

Me: Oh, you know. Dragging a 14-foot rhododendron from the front yard to the back, then digging a hole and planting it. Shoveling four semi-trucks worth of gravel and bark-o-mulch…. The usual.

Spencer: There isn't a box here for extreme gardening. I'll just put "jogging."

Spencer then gave me a plan for lifting weights to strengthen my core, which I do every other day. At least I think it's every other day. My memory isn't what it used to be.

I decided to also try out some fitness classes. The next day I showed up for a "step" aerobics class. As I was picking out a "step," a young woman with a dragon tattoo perched on her shoulder and flames shooting across her neck welcomed me. Then the instructor and took her place at the front of the room. She turned on the music. IT WAS SO LOUD MY KIDNEYS ROLLED UP INTO THE FETAL POSITION AND BEGAN TO ROCK BACK AND FORTH. MY SKIN ACTUALLY VIBRATED. MY EARS LONGED FOR THE PEACE AND QUIET OF AN AC/DC CONCERT … well, you get the idea. The music was too freaking loud.

After class, I gently pulled the instructor aside and asked her whether she always played the music so loudly. "Was it loud?" she asked. "I didn't notice."

I may not have a dragon tattoo, a flat stomach, or a dry shirt, but I am proud to say that unlike the twenty-somethings who were apparently born with earbuds and the sounds of Pitbull or Snoop Dog/Lion screeching directly into their ear canals, I can still hear. I knew joining a gym would make me feel better about myself. I was right.

## Now that's Romantic

Ah February, that most romantic of months during which we celebrate Groundhog Day (is there anything that says romance like a giant rodent?), Presidents' Day (that Abe Lincoln always makes my heart go pitter-patter, but it could be the mitral valve), and what's that other holiday called? Oh right, Valentine's Day (February 14, just in case you need a reminder).

Valentine's Day is the kind of holiday most women love because it involves frilly, girly things such as pink hearts, flowers, and getting the men in our lives to say those three little words: "I'll do dishes." Or is it "I love you"? I sometimes get those confused. Most men, on the other hand, would rather schedule an unnecessary hernia operation than try to find just the right Valentine's Day gift. Or they offer up the one present they know works every time: an unsolicited blanket apology.

Men have a point when it comes to romance – we women **DO** have unreasonable expectations. I blame fairy tales. It's hard for any man, even George Clooney and Harrison Ford (feel free to insert your own fantasy men here), to compete with a royally-attired prince on a white horse carrying a glass slipper. No matter how feminist our ideals or how independent we claim to be, when the man in our life shows up on February 14th wearing a ripped Led Zeppelin t-shirt he's had since the 70s and offers us tickets to a monster truck rally, we can't help but demand that our fairy godmother explain herself.

Where fairy tales leave off, chick flicks take over, setting even more grandiose expectations for love. I remember the year that An Officer and a Gentleman came out (1982). My husband at the time was a scrawny guy and when it became clear that no matter how much I encouraged him to drop and give me fifty he was never going to have the strength or the desire to walk into my office, scoop me into his arms, and carry me away, I was inconsolable. Where was Richard Gere when I needed him? Nor did hubby show any interest in saving me from pirates and giants (The Princess Bride), learning how to mambo (Dirty Dancing), becoming President of the U.S. to impress me (The American President), or dressing in women's lingerie to break out of a losing streak (Bull Durham). And had I put on the "display" Meg Ryan did in When Harry Met Sally, he'd have left me in the restaurant and avoided eye contact for weeks.

I've learned the hard way that it's never a good idea to take a man with you to a romantic comedy. Not only will he look bad by comparison, you'll have to go to the Bait & Tackle show the following weekend in exchange. The best date movies are those that make you feel better about the man in your life when you walk out. I suggest Dumb and Dumber, The Hangover, or my favorite of the "Boy, Will Your Man Seem Appealing" genre, Stepbrothers.

The men who suffer most during Valentine's Day are those who are married to or dating women who rarely visit the real world, opting instead for the world of romance novels. When he's lying in bed eating crackers and watching ESPN, there's no way he can live up to the steamy hype created by: "He tore open her blouse like a Publisher's Clearing House letter in which he, and some guy named Steven Bouber from Stockton, California, were potential finalists for the ten million dollar prize" or "...then he kissed her, like a butterfly kisses the windshield of a Porsche on the Autobahn."? Okay, maybe these aren't the most romantic examples, but they made me laugh.

And that, I guess is my point. For me, a guy who makes me laugh, laughs with me, and fixes the sink when it backs up is much more romantic than one who stands bare-chested, brooding on a cliff screaming my name into the wind and waves. I think most women wouldn't necessarily want to live with their ideal romantic mate day in and day out. That horse-riding prince may assume we're okay riding in back when we'd really rather have our own horse; a man who can sweep us off our feet may eventually develop back pain and be unable to pick his socks up off the floor; and a guy who can be talked into wearing a garter belt while pitching may look better in it than we do.

If we can adjust our romantic notions down a few notches and get the men in our lives to quit hoping we turn into lingerie models overnight, Valentine's Day should work out just fine. Now pass me the chocolate and no one gets hurt.

## I've Got the Moves like Rover

Every athlete has "moves." Gymnasts have back handsprings, round-offs, and lay-outs (not to be confused with lay-downs, which only happen when the coach yells too much and the team decides to play possum until he settles down). Ice skaters have double axels and triple salchows and quadruple shots of espresso in order to get up at 4 a.m. to hit the ice. Divers have pikes, tucks and pulling their swimsuits back up. In order to become really good at a sport, all athletes have to master the moves of their sport.

Now I've never really thought about dog-wrangling as a sport. It's not, for example, included in either the summer or winter Olympics, which is a darned shame because imagine how much more fun synchronized swimming or bobsledding would be with dogs involved. But as someone who has been wrangling wiener dogs for 30 years now, it occurs to me that anyone living with canines, especially of the smaller variety, has moves of his or her own. They may not be moves like Jagger, but then neither are Mick's these days.

If you're a dog-wrangler yourself, see if any of these moves seem familiar to you:

**The Hover** – This is done when I attempt to exit the sofa or bed (assuming the canines have allowed me on the furniture that day). Any time I attempt to put my feet on the floor, I must first hover them several inches above the floor in case a dachshund decides that he or she must be in that exact spot at that very nanosecond. I have been known to hover for a full 15 seconds as my dogs take turns occupying all spots on the floor in which my feet might land.

The hover is made more difficult when done on hardwood floors in stocking feet—and of course, I am not allowed to wear shoes in the house for fear of stepping on a paw or a tail and not realizing it. On several occasions, a hover move has gone wrong and I have ended up doing the splits, which is not a recommended move for dog-wranglers over 40.

**The Night Hover** – This is very similar to The Hover, only it is done in pitch darkness, so I have to lower my feet to the floor slowly and in small increments because I have to sense rather than see whether a dog is beneath me. If I feel a nip on the toe, for example, I know not to put my foot down just yet.

**The Older Lady than I am Shuffle** – You can't tell from seeing me out in the real world where I walk like a mostly normal human, putting one foot in front of the other and lifting my feet slightly with each step, but I have mastered this move and am thinking of going pro. At home, I slide my feet along the floor instead of actually taking steps. That way, if contact with a canine is made, it is from below, not above. Sometimes I find myself at the grocery store or walking down the sidewalk dog-free, and I have to remind myself to lift my feet. Thankfully, I've watched America's Top Model a few times, so I just pretend I'm doing a runway walk—this explains the pouty face I gave before executing turns.

**The Iron Cross** – You may know this as a move in which a male gymnast extends both arms straight out while on the rings, his body suspended in mid-air for at least two seconds. Although the arm position is the same, in dog-wrangling, the Iron Cross is done with feet firmly planted on the ground (or hovering, depending on circumstances). With one or more leashes in each hand, the Iron Cross may occur any time one dog on one leash spots a squirrel heading in one direction while another dog on another leash spots a cat heading in the other. Whenever I successfully complete this move, I give myself a cookie.

**The Mummy Unwrapped** – Whenever one sleeps surrounded by dogs who may be under or on top of a sheet, a blanket, and a comforter and there are at least four pillows in the bed (in my case, one for the human's head, one for under or between the human's knees, one for the dog who like scrunching for an hour before settling in, and one for the dog who believes she is a princess), getting up three or four times every night for bathroom breaks is akin to unwrapping a mummy from the inside. I have found that this move is made more difficult by the requirement to not awaken any sleeping hounds lest they decide that 2:17 a.m. would be a great time to have breakfast and not roll over anyone's tail, including my own.

I guess what I'm getting at here is that if you live with dogs, no matter how sloth-like you may feel sometimes, you're really an athlete, so give yourself some credit! Just be sure when you've finished reading this column and want to get a drink, that you do The Hover and perhaps The Older Lady than I am Shuffle.

## I Won't Ballroom Dance, Don't Ask Me

I love watching ballroom dancing. The graceful movement, the teamwork between partners, the costumes that are so over-the-top they give Lady Gaga ideas for her next red carpet look… Ballroom dancing is art, really. But just as with art, the world is better off with me as a spectator than a participant.

Synchronized partner dancing is not my thing and it's not just because I may be the world's largest klutz. (I know some of you out there are vying for the title, but until you have accidentally glued your forearms together AND stabbed yourself in the neck with a corncob holder in the same day, don't even think about challenging me.) My issue with ballroom dancing is more about the fact that when I hear great music, I don't want to have to think about anything or anyone except expressing myself, wildly and unabashedly. I'm not in the mood to think about whether I'm following or leading – I've been told that I tend to do the latter, no matter what the circumstances. And I don't want to have to worry about whose foot I will mangle if I don't get the next turn executed properly or whose sacroiliac is going to be out of joint because I don't dip well.

May I digress for a moment? Whose idea was "dipping" anyway? According to my secret sources (Wikipedia and answers.com, the source of all truth in the universe), the waltz was created in Austria in 1776. So while our forefathers were setting out the rights and responsibilities we are still arguing about today, the Austrians were putting on their dancing shoes. Interestingly, back then the shoes of both men and women were heeled. Doesn't it just make you feel better to know at some point men had to dance in heels too? Although not recorded in the annals of on-line history, I'm fairly certain that after a few years, the men started to get tired of being dragged out by their wives to boogey every Saturday night, not to mention how much their feet hurt. So a few of them got together and decided to prank the ladies by creating "the dip," a dangerous back pain-inducing move that was meant to dissuade the gals from dancing, but instead lead an onlooker to invent chiropractic and rake in the big bucks, er, Kronen.

Okay, back to my point, if I can remember what it was…

Oh, yes. I recently went to hear one of my favorite local bands play at an event promoted for "boomers." The great thing about dances for boomers is you are almost guaranteed that there will be no hip hop dancing or crunking. Not to mention I knew that I would be among the youngest people there and therefore experience a boost in my self-esteem. I should also probably mention here that the event started at 7 p.m. Bonus!

I sidled up to the bar and ordered my usual – a glass of fizzy water. Yes, that's the kind of party animal I am. Then I took a seat at a table next to the dance floor and watched as a dozen couples whirled and twirled each other around like gray-haired auditioners for So You Think You Can Dance. They were all fantastic and I felt more than a little intimidated and out of my element. Unfortunately, the fizzy water didn't do anything to ease my nerves nor did the woman who politely pointed out to me that my blouse was on inside out.

When I returned from addressing my wardrobe malfunction in the ladies' room, I noticed a handful of younger women (defined as "close to my age") dancing with each other near the stage. They danced in a circle, not paired up, and their moves were wild and free. Just as I was about to ask them if I could join their group, a guy tapped me on the shoulder and invited me to dance. My heart pounded. Partly because I was happy to know I've still got it (only it's located slightly further south than it used to be), but mostly because I did not want try to keep up with the professional dancers on the floor. I agreed to dance with him, but pointed to the ballroom dancers and said, "I don't dance like that."

"How do you dance?" he asked.

I pointed to the wild women near the stage. "Like that."

"That's not dancing," he harrumphed. "That's Jazzercise."

Guess who I danced with? That's right, the ladies. It was great. And by the end of the evening, there were about thirty women all shaking our booties without having to walk backward and tuck under a gentleman's arm. Not that there's anything wrong with that, but sometimes a girl's gotta do what a girl's gotta do. And in this case, it didn't include dipping.

**I'm Pro-Aging**

Anyone who watches any television at all must believe that most women over 30 spend 95% of their time trying to reduce the appearance of fine lines and wrinkles and lengthen and restore their eyelashes. If I see 20-year-olds hawking anti-aging creams or that model with the shiny eyelashes long enough to get caught in her earrings one more time, I may just have to get Botox to rid myself of the semi-permanent scowl these commercials have caused

We're all a little vain -- I DID comb my hair before leaving the house this morning and check to make sure my skirt was NOT tucked in my pantyhose -- but imagine if we freed up all that time to do more important things such as demand no one interfere in our right to reproductive health care, buy up all the Etch-a-Sketches and put them up for sale on e-Bay, or even just breathe. Breathing is really good; I highly recommend it. Of course, you may have to take off your body control garments or control top pantyhose to get the full benefits. I imagine breathing probably would make lashes grow too.

Every study I've read shows that anti-aging creams don't work, yet there's a new one promising us miracles every few weeks or so. *"You'll look 65% younger if viewed from 10 feet or more in low light while wearing something so revealing no one will be able to focus on your face."* Or some such nonsense. I'm tempted to bottle up some Oregon rain, toss in a little moss for color and authenticity, and sell it as an anti-aging mist. It sure does keep my skin moist through most of the fall and winter. And spring. And summer. I have 55 gallons of the stuff in my rain barrel and all I have to do is climb on my roof for the moss.

The research on growing new eyelashes says it can be done, but only if we're willing to accept itching, redness, eye color change, and lashes that look like squashed tarantulas every time we put on our reading glasses. I've never heard anyone tell me why insufficient eyelashes are a problem. If so, why don't men need to worry. Or is it okay that they comb their ear hair over their eyes?

By the way, there are disadvantages to too-long eyelashes. I wore my first fake eyelashes while dressed as Lucille Ball and keynoting an "I Love Lucy"-themed conference recently. At one point, I blinked and the 2" lashes obstructed my vision temporarily, long enough for me to pitch forward off the stage. Boy, did I have 'splainin' to do after that.

Forget wasting your money. Just toss a towel over the mirror if you must and make friends with people who could care less how deep your lines are or whether you have lashes long enough to swat away flies. Or, if you really want to spend some money, I've got some mossy anti-aging water just for you. After all, trees never look a day over 50.

**Summer Vacation**

"Summer vacation!" Are there any two words in the English language that bring more joy to children and inner children alike? Sure "Free candy" and "Puppies here!" come close, but looking forward to long sunny days spent doing next to nothing is about as close to nirvana as life gets.

It's been years (okay, let's be truthful here, it's been decades) since I had an entire summer free to do whatever I chose. Still something deep inside me expects that as soon as I flip the calendar page from May to June, all the joys of a childhood summer are going to be mine to indulge in once again. My inner child gets restless, and I don't think it's just because she's had too much coffee and chocolate.

As soon as the days warm up, I want to put on a bathing suit and run through the sprinkler on the front lawn. Sure the neighbors would laugh at me out there in my tummy control Hello Kitty swimsuit and four layers of zinc oxide on all my exposed body parts, but someone's got to keep the cul-de-sac entertained. And I'm just the girl for the job.

I don't want to stop with the sprinkler, though. I want to hurl my body down a Slip-n-Slide with all the other kids. I resist only because I don't have the type of insurance that would cover the broken bones and bruised organs I'm sure I'd suffer as a result. And I'm fairly certain "acting immaturely" is considered a pre-existing condition.

I want to hang upside down by my knees from a giant oak tree too. Unfortunately, the last time I tried it a few summers ago, I learned the hard way that getting up is much easier than getting down. I was stuck on that branch for seven or eight minutes as I tried to figure out how to gracefully extricate myself from my bat-like position without suffering permanent head injury. It was a little embarrassing, but having all that blood rush to my head really brought back a lot of old memories. They weren't necessarily my memories; many of them seemed to involve chimpanzees and giant tree sloths. Ah, my ancestors!

And of course I want to chase down the ice cream truck and buy five popsicles with my babysitting money and eat them all before they can melt. Nothing says summer better than blue lips and brain freeze. (By the way, wouldn't Blue Lips and Brain Freeze make a great name for a Jimmy Buffet cover band?

I was a nerdy girl who loved going to school, but even I knew there were some things you could only learn during summer vacation – like how to water ski. Despite being legally blind without my glasses and getting entangled in a fishing line and almost hitting the side of a bridge, my inner child recalls fondly that first day I managed to stand up on a pair of skis on a crystal blue lake. I'm assuming it was crystal blue; I couldn't actually see it. The wind whipped through my wet hair as I soared behind the boat, fishhooks and bait flying behind me.

There were lessons in making homemade ice cream by rolling a can filled with sweet cream back and forth on a beach towel for hours until all the kids gave up and decided to make S'mores over the Hibachi instead. But we still managed to save enough room for ice cream when the grown-ups – whose tolerance for tedium was much higher than ours was – finally popped the lid off the can and scooped out frosted deliciousness into our bowls.

Let's not forget the lessons in love that summer also brings. There was that one July in high school when I met my first true love Danny while hanging out at the beach with my friends Rizzo and Frenchy… oh, wait, that wasn't my life, that was Grease. None of my childhood summers involved tight leather pants and singing duets with greasy-haired guys. But you know what, that would be the perfect summer activity for me this year since the Slip-n-Slide and tree-hanging are out. I wonder if they make breathable vegan leather pants that won't cause me to pass out when I have a hot flash. I should Google that.

## Women's Wisdom

Forget the agricultural and industrial revolutions (if you haven't already). Humanity's progress throughout the millennia has been due in large part to the wisdom of "Old Wives' Tales" or to be more politically correct, "Wisdom from Married, Partnered, Single, Widowed, or Divorced Women Who Have Been Around for A While but Due to Healthy Eating, Regular Exercise, and Occasional Botox Injections Don't Look Their Ages."

These tidbits of practical information seemed to morph out of thin air. You may have heard, "Never go outside with wet hair because you'll catch a cold" or "If you roll your eyes at me one more time, they're going to get stuck in the back of your head" from your mother, but chances are, she heard it from her own mother, and so on and so on. No one knows which woman originally birthed these tips, but I like to think her name was Nakjtnebtepnefer (which means "beautiful and strong champion" in ancient Egyptian) and she was the first woman scribe in Thebes in 1423 B.C., a role she achieved by posing as a man named Bakole (which means "help me build the house"). Not that I've given it much thought.

To this day, I still believe that drinking coffee stunts your growth (I was the only one of my female siblings who avoided it until my 30s and I am the only one over 5'2"—by a whopping 5"), that sitting too close to the television will make you go blind, and that all your body heat and most of your memory escapes through the top of your head. The best part about women's wisdom is that much of it has been proven correct by science. Eating carrots does help eyesight; an apple a day can keep the doctor away; stepping on a crack may not break your mother's back, but if she finds out you did it just to see if it would, she will ground you; and ghosts don't haunt children who remember to wash behind their ears. Okay, maybe that last one was more of a family superstition, but I dare science to prove it wrong.

Unfortunately, most women these days are too busy working, raising families, running for president, and pinning things on Pinterest to have time to create new words of wisdom for the ages. That's a darn shame, if you ask me because as time and technology march on, someone needs to warn young 'ens of what to avoid to make it through life in the 21st century. Fortunately, my family of canines is asleep on the sofa, and I had to stop pinning things on Pinterest because apparently, according to the intervention my dogs held, "I was becoming an addict." So I'm here to provide pithy and relevant advice for the coming generations. They can roll their eyes at me later.

Here we go:

1. Keep your friends close and your Twitter followers as far away as possible.
2. When you unhinge your jaw to take a bite out of a giant hamburger, it will stay unhinged for life.
3. Never pierce a body part that causes you to whistle when you breathe.
4. Stay in school—preferably kindergarten where you can nap and eat cookies.
5. If you hunch over your cell phone texting all day, you'll end up like Igor from Young Frankenstein ("Hump? What hump?")
6. Every time you mutter "*whatever*" under your breath at your parents or teachers, a puppy whimpers.
7. If it feels good, chances are there will be consequences to pay.
8. Don't take your laptop in a gas station bathroom.
9. Never wear flannel pajamas in public after Easter.
10. Every hair you rip out will grow back twice as thick and in a really inconvenient place in your next life.
11. If you're still living at home, you're too young to "have work done."
12. Just because all the other kids are getting their eyelids tattooed doesn't mean you have to.
13. There is no such thing as too much chocolate.
14. Astonish your friends; learn to sign your name using cursive writing.

15. When you lie, someone will post a video on YouTube of what you actually said and did.
16. You'll never go very far with your pants hanging around your mid-thighs.
17. Feed a cold, scarve a Bieber.
18. If "reality TV star" is your career goal, you need a plan B, C, and D.
19. Never marry anyone your dog disapproves of.
20. Stop painting dirty hieroglyphics on your grandfather's pyramid or you'll be reincarnated as a mule.

   That's all the "wisdom" this divorced woman who has been around for a while due to mostly healthy eating, regular exercise, extremely good genes, avoiding coffee and stepping on cracks has to offer for today. I hope it helps.

## There's a Coupon for That

I've always been a coupon clipper – or, more accurately these days, a coupon-ripper-outer. Sadly, my good scissors can no longer cut paper. Apparently I wasn't supposed to use them to trim the artificial grass I glued to my new outdoor doggy ramp. This was the same project that resulted in my right bicep being semi-permanently glued to my left forearm… But I digress.

Now, where was I? Oh, yes.

Lately, coupons scare me. Not the ones that show up in the newspaper on Sunday – those I love. It's fun sitting down with the coupon section of the paper and a nice hot cup of decaf coffee (of course I drink decaf; I'm the sort of person who glues her own arms together. Clearly I should not be allowed near caffeine). I can take my time as I sort through the colorful ads for pants with a waist that adjusts after dinner and lifelike cat figurines to find a 50-cent discount on my favorite brand of cereal. It's my version of a treasure hunt.

The "target-specific" coupons we all stuff in our brought-from-home grocery bags at the end of a shopping expedition are proof that Big Brother is here and he knows what we eat. It's one thing to quickly fill up your shopping cart with vegetarian chili and Beano, but quite another to have written documentation of your odd culinary habits. Doesn't it bother you that someone somewhere knows who you really are and how often you load up on peanut butter and shave your legs? Those are just randomly chosen examples, by the way. Not in the least a clue to my shopping behavior.

Believe it or not, I'm kind of a private person. I don't tweet each time I change hairstyles or spouses (I believe at this point I've had one more hairstyle than spouse). If I'm leaving for a four-day vacation in Mexico, I'm not going to post it on Facebook, primarily because my dogs would never let me go on vacation. And I usually only share the deep intimate secrets of my life with my closest friends – and all of you reading this book. Even so, there are some things I'd rather keep a secret from everyone, such as the fact that it only took me one day last week to polish off a box of gingersnaps and a half-dozen popsicles. The coupon people, however, already know.

Don't get me wrong, I'm thankful for the savings on items I use regularly and am not embarrassed to let the world know about. The almond milk, the sustainable laundry detergent, the whole wheat spaghetti… I appreciate financial assistance in purchasing those. But do I really need two coupons for hair dye spitting out at me every time I check out, letting the cashier and anyone else within ten feet know that I am not the natural redhead I pretend to be? It's almost humiliating enough to make me revert to my natural hair color.

I find it scary to think that some computer programmer sitting in a dark room playing Grand Theft Auto XXIV can profile me in seconds flat. "Yeah, officer, she likes to think she's healthy, what with all the low-fat, organic stuff, but according to our records of popsicle and cookie purchases, she's probably ten pounds heavier than she claims on her driver's license. Plus, it's been 93 days since she last dyed her roots, and from the bandages and rubbing alcohol she bought last week, she may have just glued her arms together. She should be easy to spot."

As bad as the truth is when it stares us in the face, it's even worse when the coupons that print out don't seem to know us at all. Or do they? I've gotten three fish oil supplement coupons in the past month. Does the coupon programmer think I need to get an echocardiogram? And what's with the baby food discounts? Do not tell me I'm preg ... no, that's not even possible. Whew, for a second there I could feel my blood pressure skyrocket. Oh, maybe that was the plan. They thought they could scare me into buying fish oil tablets for my heart. Well, it probably wouldn't hurt.

I guess there's only one thing a privacy-loving, coupon-ripping gal can do – subvert coupon technology. From now on, I'm going to purchase all my non-essentials and hair dye from the mom and pop drugstore down the street. They don't have coupon people, so there won't be any hard evidence to prove I've committed any grocery crimes. Take that, Big Brother!

## The Wiener Dogs' Perspective on Halloween

Halloween may be one of the most popular holidays for human kids and adults, but from what I can tell, it ranks second only to July 4$^{th}$ as the most annoying holiday for canines. Let's check in with my three dachshunds, Penny, Watson and Justin to see just how much they don't love All Hallows Eve.

Penny: No, I will not wear this Batgirl outfit, no matter how many cookies you give me. (By the way – what happened to those peanut butter ones? I liked those better. They were easier to chew and they tasted like peanut butter! Have you ever had peanut butter? It is, for lack of a better word, amazing!) I am not a Batgirl. I am a dachshund and this costume makes me look ridiculous… and a little chubby. Besides, do I look like the kind of dog who would be seen in a flimsy cape? I think not. Take it off me or you will find a surprise in your closet later.

Watson: There are humans at the door. Mom! Send them away, we were napping peacefully and they're interrupting our sleep. Hey, what is that you're giving them from that giant bowl? Are there treats in there? Why do strangers who bother us when we're just settling in for the evening get treats, while we, your loyal and trusted companions get bupkus? Come on come on come on come on… can't you see I want a treat? Look at these eyes. Hear this tail thumping against the door despite the fact that I have to bark every three seconds at my highest pitch to make sure the humans know they are not welcome here? Send them away and give me that bowl. You won't be sorry.

Justin: Yawn. What's going on? Why is no one on the sofa now? Who won final Jeopardy?

Penny: I don't care if you think dogs in costumes are cute. And no, I don't want to match your outfit. You should have just dressed up like a wiener dog and avoided all this stress. No, it doesn't help when you show me pictures of other dogs on Facebook who seem to enjoy dressing up for Halloween. If you ask me, they need therapy. Or peanut butter. A little peanut butter helps with almost everything.

Justin: Did someone say dinner? I swore I heard the word dinner. I'm going to mosey into the kitchen just to be sure.

Watson: OHMYDOG! There are a ghost, two princesses and a robot at the front door! I shall protect us! Barkbarkbarkbarkwagwagwagwag! Why are they not scared of me? I intimidate both the UPS guy and the meter reader with my fearsomeness, but these small humans don't seem to care. And why are you giving them more treats? Look at those bags and pillowcases filled with yummies. Have you not heard of childhood obesity? I will step up and help you fight it by eating all the rest of the treats. It will be tough, but I'm willing.

Justin: Hey, I may not be able to see well any more but I know that's a cowboy hat you've just put on my head. I'll show you what I think of it by shredding it with my teeth. I'll go into my bed and do that now. But you let me know if there's going to be dinner. Announce it loudly so that I can hear over all the racket.

Watson: Did you know there's a pumpkin that seems to be on fire right outside the front door? Do you need me to go outside and pee on it? I could do that. It would only take two of whatever is in that big bowl.

Penny: No, I am also not going to pretend to be a witch so you can wear that witch hat. Despite what you may have heard, I'm a D-O-G… and you haven't used a broom in several weeks, if we're being totally honest.

Watson: The knocking. The incessant knocking. It never ends, does it? Every time I go get a drink of water to quench my throat which is parched from all the barking, the knocking starts then the barking then the begging for treats then the not getting any treats. This is exhausting. Why don't we just turn out the lights and pretend no one's home like we do when your ex drops by? Then we could have all the treats in the bowl to ourselves.

Justin: z-z-z-z-z…

Watson: Wait, the treats are all gone? How is that even possible? Hey, how many did you have?

Penny: I may have eaten the Batgirl cape. It did NOT taste like peanut butter, just so you know.

## What to Wear, What to Wear?

It has come to my attention recently that I am 57-1/2 years old. At least that's what it says on my birth certificate. But it's auf Deutsch, so I may be translating it wrong.

I don't think much about my age (or my weight or how many calories were in that giant molasses cookie I devoured a few minutes ago), but two days ago when a girlfriend who is m-u-c-h younger than I invited me to drinks, my first thought was "What does a woman my age wear to down a few margaritas on a Saturday night?"

The truth is I don't often drink, even though I regularly perform comedy in bars. When I'm performing, I know what to wear – something bold enough for stand-up yet stretchy enough to do improv in without showing the audience anything they don't want to see.

For the celebratory drinks, which I knew we would consume on an outdoor patio in the 90-degree heat, I chose to wear a sheer green blouse with a black bra underneath and hot pink short shorts. I was going for "cool" as in "something I won't sweat through before the drinks arrive."

When I arrived, my girlfriend (did I mention that she is m-u-c-h younger than me, as in, I could be her mother if I'd gotten knocked up at 16) nodded approvingly. "Look at the hot mama!" I glanced behind me, as I do any time anyone gives me a compliment, just to be sure before responding. "Me?"

We drank our margaritas with a few other friends. I am a cheap drunk (I often end up getting married when tipsy) and within a few minutes I admitted to the group the subconscious reason behind my outfit. The truth is I tend to shed clothing when drinking (yes, I know it's not only a cliché, it's a country western song – Margaritas Make Her Clothes Fall Off), so I'd chosen the one blouse in my closet that is most difficult to remove. And the hot pants? Well, the shorter the shorts, the less likely it is that anyone will stare at my knees, which on a good day, look like a pair of Grumpy Cats velcroed to the front of my legs.

Have you ever wondered how much more room women would have in our brains if we got back all the brain cells destroyed by all the times we have tried to choose an outfit to suit an occasion? If an entire part of our brain wasn't devoted to making sure we didn't look fat or old or like a hussy, we'd probably be able to negotiate world peace and cure heart disease with an amazing peach pie. Or at least remember where we parked.

I occasionally watch a television show called Tiny House Nation, in which couples or families move into houses that are 300 square feet or smaller. They are forced to part with most of their belongings, including most of their wardrobe. I think one of the reasons I enjoy the show is the idea that if I only had two outfits in my closet, my daily decisions would be so much easier.

But for now, rather than paring my wardrobe down to almost nothing, I think I'll just lay off the alcohol instead. That way I can keep my fashion secrets to my almost 58-year-old self. Better just to let them think I'm a hot mama.

## Meditate on This

I can't meditate. I've taken workshops and read books. I've even stalked people who were wearing yoga pants to see if a little of their calming spirit would rub off on me. Unfortunately, even peacefully minded people get a little agitated if you slide into their passenger seat and start peppering them with questions about their aura.

In my quest for nirvana (the state of mind, not the band), I've filled my house with accessories meant to help me get into the mood. Sitting in the middle of my kitchen table is a wind chime that was crafted to evoke a peaceful mind and body. Unfortunately, the chimes are buried under bills, the leaves from the schefflera I keep forgetting to water, winter scarves I haven't gotten around to putting away yet, half-eaten dog toys with missing squeakers, and notes to myself to organize and de-clutter. On a nearby shelf hangs a small gong I bought to signal the beginning and end of my meditation exercises. Unfortunately, every time I strike it, the dogs bark and run to the windows thinking we have guests who could possibly have cookies or maybe a squirrel in their pockets.

In my guest bedroom is a miniature zen sand garden complete with tiny rake. The act of raking the sand around the rocks is supposed to help relieve stress and release worries. I've only used it once and afterward, I had to vacuum sand out of the carpet for days. I'm hoping my guests have better luck, although one recently left a note saying the sand trap was a nice touch but she couldn't find a miniature golf club to hit her ball out.

My home office is adorned with a lovely framed reminder that all I need to do today is breathe in and breathe out. As you undoubtedly know, breathing is important in meditation. I've also found that it is important in staying alive. The problem is that when I become aware of my breathing – as meditation instructors tell us to do – it makes me a little paranoid. I start worrying about my poor brain and how it has to remember to tell my lungs to inhale and exhale every couple of seconds. What if it forgets for a few hours? What if I'm trying to remember the name of a friend or where I left my keys and my brain becomes overwhelmed and just shuts down? Needless to say, this kind of thinking is not conducive to feeing at peace with the universe. Or even with my own body parts.

And forget clearing my mind. Whenever I try, my brain becomes a pan of Jiffy Pop popcorn. One kernel of a thought becomes seven, which heats things up and then there are dozens, then hundreds, until finally my brain is about to explode out of its aluminum foil wrapper. I'm supposed to be focusing on being and nothingness, not wondering if I should use Facebook to look up the boy I stole a potholder loop from in the third grade so I can apologize. Instead of living in the moment, I end up reliving my entire life, with particular emphasis on the 80s.

I also tend to giggle at the word Kundalini. I just can't help myself.

But about a month ago the miraculous happened. I was attending a concert at an outdoor concert with a friend. We arrived an hour early and scoped out a nice spot for our blanket on the lawn and she left to get something to eat. I decided to lie down until she got back. With my hat over my eyes, I could hear people talking and laughing, babies crying, and the sounds of footsteps on the concrete steps nearby. Plastic containers of food were opened and my olfactory senses were flooded with the smells of fresh fruits and tasty dinners. The sun was hot and beat down on my reclining body. Suddenly, in the midst of this overload of stimulation, I achieved nirvana. Perhaps it was because I was lying in what is known in yoga as "corpse position" (this, by the way, is not your usual chalk outline position.) As it turns out, I don't need peace and quiet to meditate; I need cacophony.

Then Lyle Lovett took the stage and I moved from nirvana to heaven. Ommmmmm.

## The Hollow Dog

Between the table
And the chairs
Between the dishes
And the floor
Falls the snack

*For mine is the kitchen*

Between the recipe
And the creation
Between the begging
And the response
Falls the snack

*Food is very good*

Between the desire
And the rumblings
Between the sad eyes
And the beseeching
Falls the Snack

*For mine is the kitchen*

*This is the way the dinner ends*
*This is the way the dinner ends*
*This is the way the dinner ends*
*Not with a howl but a whimper.*

## Naked and (Somewhat) Unafraid

When I signed up for a nude group photo with 100 women, I did so for a few reasons: the photographer is amazing; the women's empowerment message of the shoot is something I care deeply about and at 57-1/2 years-old (yes, I count half years now), the chances of anyone asking me to pose naked would surely fall off soon. From 1 to 0, I'm thinking.

I am not an exhibitionist. I'm okay with my body – I just look better with certain bits camouflaged by clothing, belts, scarves, mirrors, detour signs, tequila, etc.

I've never skinny dipped or flashed. I do occasionally walk around naked in my house, but usually just from the shower to the bedroom and I apologize to my wiener dogs if they seem scared.

Needless to say, the idea of my stripping down past my skivvies with a roomful of other women was a daunting challenge for me. I thought about backing out several times as the day loomed closer. But as uncomfortable as I may be with my own nudity, I'm more uncomfortable with hypocrisy. To chicken out of a women's empowerment event because I'm a too scared would just not do. I threw my shoulders back, sucked in my post-menopausal poochy belly and headed to the site of the event.

I arrived a few minutes early at the warehouse where we would all meet, strip, apply mud all over our bodies, and then walk approximately ¼ mile to an open field where the photo shoot would happen. (I arrive everywhere a few minutes early—be forewarned, those of you who end up planning my funeral.) There were about 25 women there already, including one who was very pregnant. I let my tummy relax. The women were all dressed and there was an open bar of sorts. From the number of women drinking and standing in line for the one bathroom, clearly I wasn't the only nervous one.

One of my former radio co-hosts was there, as was one of my closest friends, a woman who is much younger and in much better shape than I am and yet I invited her anyway. She posted on FB that it was about time she got a chance to see my boobs.

I recognized a few other faces in the crowd. One came up to me and told me she had taken grammar from me at the university. "And now you're going to see me naked. And you're going to know I have a tramp stamp," I tittered. Everyone laughed. She said, "I knew you were cool." And she did it grammatically correctly.

More women arrived, including one with a newborn baby. A few men were there too, photographers and friends/boyfriends/lovers/spouses of women. They were enlisted in stirring the tub and kiddy pool filled with red mud that we would soon be coating our bodies with outside the warehouse in the middle of a Saturday afternoon like a poor-woman's version of a spa treatment.

Finally the moment arrived and the disrobing began. Little by little the shirts, skirts, pants, bras, and panties came off of the 50 or so women who had made it past their nerves and into the door of the warehouse. Many of us then wrapped back up in robes or towels as we stood in line for our mud armor. Slowly, everyone shed not only their clothes, but their inhibitions. There were beautiful bodies everywhere – skinny and pudgy, white and brown, young and not-so-young.

Watching the women before us help each other pour mud on themselves and rub in all over was awe-inspiring. Not only did we look tribal, but we felt like a tribe – of strong, carefree women ready to take back power from anyone who tries to control what we do with our own bodies. Our laughter moved from girlish giggles to deep throaty laughs of self-assured women. We are woman, hear us grunt and snort with laughter while playing in a kiddy pool of mud!

When it was my turn, two women I'd never met rubbed mud all over me. As a redhead, I've never had a real tan and this is the closest I've come. I caught the eye of the other gingers and we were all pleased to finally have a skin color that couldn't reflect moonlight.

While we were mudding up, several men drove along the fence separating the warehouse parking lot from a nearby storage facility.

They honked and did what men would do when confronted suddenly and unexpectedly with many, many naked women. I'm fairly certain a few imagined themselves in a *52-some*, but it didn't matter. What would have been uncomfortable and creepy on our own was all part of the fun because we were with our tribe.

Then began the long, barefooted walk down across a major street and down a side street, across from a chocolate store (very fitting and had I not been naked and muddy, I might have stopped in) and finally into a field. Let me reiterate: Except for a coating of red mud, we walked naked, en masse, stopping dozens of cars, seeing people leer and almost drive off the road. None of it mattered. We were a tribe. And despite the mud, many of our tribal tattoos were still visible. It was the first time my lower back butterfly flew free outside.

Once in the field, we laughed and kvetched about animal poop below and clouds overhead that threatened rain. When given the instruction, we ran like a pack of female wolves, then we walked back and did it again and again. Someone took a vote and we discovered I was the oldest woman there. A cheer went up from the tribe. That alone, being cheered for being the eldest, is such a rare and amazing gift, I want to re-wrap it an give it to myself on every birthday.

After six takes, the photographer was happy with the results and we marched back, repeating our audacious hike, only this time, slightly less nervous and with slightly less mud (much had rubbed off while running across the field six times and brushing up against each other as we tried to stay close enough together for the photos).

Back at the warehouse, some women showered under a cold hose. My friend hula hooped naked because how many opportunities do you get to do that? I rubbed as much mud off as I could with my hands, put on my robe, said goodbye to my new clan and headed home. I was secretly hoping to get pulled over and have to explain my attire–muddy hair and nails and fluffy periwinkle house robe.

When I got home, the dogs thought the remaining mud tasted delicious.

I'm proud that I didn't allow nerves, modesty, or an overactive bladder talk me out of this glorious experience. Who knows what's next? Is there such thing as naked stand-up comedy?

**The Big Bark Theory:  Fido Explains the Universe**

In an effort to finally clear up the whole creation versus evolution debate, I decided to ask my dog, Justin. Here's what he had to say:

*Me:    So how did the universe get its start?*

*Justin:*  In the beginning there was Dog. Dog was a loving animal (as all dogs are), but she was lonely. She had no pack to run with, no one to lead, no one whose slippers she could shred. Every night, Dog would howl into that great chasm of space, in the general direction of where there should be a moon. She'd howl for hours, hoping someone would hear her and come out to play.

One night, instead of howling, Dog barked. It was a Big Bark. It was the biggest bark the universe had ever heard.

Since the universe had never heard such a big bark before, it quivered. Its hackles stood on end. And finally, it shook its loose floppy skin over and over again. And, as it shook, all sorts of stuff came out in every direction -- stuff that formed stars, stuff that formed planets, stuff that just dripped all over the floor of the universe.

When Dog finally stopped barking, she saw what she had done and she said to herself, "I need a nap." So she snoozed for a couple of eons (that's fourteen eons in dog years).  And that's that.

*Me:  Did evolution play a role?*

*Justin:*  Actually, it was revolution. After the Big Bark, the earth was a cold and unfriendly planet. The only life that could be found was that present in Dog's drool, and it wasn't the kind of life you'd want to invite over for supper. And, as she napped, Dog drooled all over the universe.

When Dog finally awoke, she looked around for someone to play with. Was there anyone with opposable thumbs who could throw a stick for her?

No. Was there anyone she could chase up a tree? No. Was there anyone with a great-smelling hindquarters for her to sniff? No. Nothing but amoebae and paramecium, and, as far as Dog could tell, they didn't even have hindquarters.

Dog got bored. She began to chase her tail. She chased it 'round and 'round, faster and faster until the planets and stars started to spin around her. Eventually, all this spinning kicked up a lot of space dust, which caused Dog to sneeze and to stop chasing her tail.

Finally, when the dust cleared on Earth and a few other planets -- Mars, Jupiter and the planet Alpo -- life had revolved. In fact, it continued to revolve for several minutes, causing most of it to be just a little queasy when things finally settled down.

Now, you're probably wondering what that life looked like. Well, I'll tell you. There were three life forms. The highest, the form created in the image of Dog, called, you're never gonna believe this -- dog; the middle life form, the one capable of opening cans and tossing Frisbees -- human; and the lowest life form, the one that was a pure freak of nature -- cat.

*Me: How old is the universe?*

*Justin:* Older than those leftovers in the back of your refrigerator.

*Me: Is the universe expanding or contracting?*

*Justin:* It depends on whether it has just eaten.

*Me: Which galaxy is closest to us?*

*Justin:* For most of us, that would be a Ford Galaxy. Which, by the way, is an excellent car to stick your head out of because it doesn't usually go faster than 30 m.p.h.

*Me: What is the Big Dipper?*

*Justin:* The appropriate amount of food for a dog over 50 lbs. The Little Dipper, of course, is for smaller dogs and those on a diet.

*Me: What is the Milky Way?*

*Justin:* The Milky Way is the only galaxy in which you can find Milk Bones.

*ME: Why is there gravity?*

*Justin:* So that things fall onto the floor where dogs can eat them.

*Me: What were the first words spoken on the moon?*

*Justin:* "One small step for man -- one long way to go to walk the dog."

*Me: What is the speed of light?*

*Justin:* Way too fast. You stick your head out the window and your ears would blow right off.

Then, Justin rolled over on his back and demanded that I pet his stomach. I had many more questions, but he immediately fell asleep. I guess he felt I'd learned enough for one day.

## Getting Healthy Can Wear You Out

I've been a health nut since for years. For more than a decade, I ran the health promotion department at a major university in the Lone Star State, where I tried to convince Texans that eating a 2-lb. chicken-fried steak smothered in gravy while drinking beer and smoking a cigar wasn't necessarily a good thing—especially for breakfast.

Not that long ago the rules for keeping healthy were fairly simply: eat less, exercise more, stop smoking, and make sure your 10-gallon hat didn't fall into your eyes while driving your cattle into town. There is SO much more to it now.

We're supposed to get all kinds of regular medical tests. If you're over 40, you should have an annual exam and a mammogram or a prostate exam (never both, unless you're overly cautious or a prankster). You also need to have your eyes checked, your teeth cleaned, your blood counted (1, 2, 3, 8.5 million…), your cholesterol tested, your moles scanned, and your bank account resuscitated. After you've peed in a cup, spit in a tube, showed your backside to strangers in the waiting room of the clinic, and filled out all your paperwork, you can buy tickets to Dr. Oz where you can don purple gloves and feel someone else's liver.

Once you know everything about what's going on inside you, you need to change your diet. Chances are, even if you're a gluten-free, lactose-free, vegetarian who only eats food that is organic, free-range and comes to you via bicycle messenger on nights with a full moon, you're doing something wrong. Have you replaced all your grains with those the Mayans grew, including quinoa, amaranth, and spelt? (By the way, my spell checker does NOT like the word 'spelt.') Do your tomatoes come in a can (a big no-no) or some other healthier container such as a knapsack or pair of tube socks? Is there kale in your salad? And if so, did you massage it before putting it on the table because apparently kale needs to be relaxed and stress-free before being consumed. Perhaps a little Enya music with lunch would help. Seaweed is also on the list, but I don't know whether it needs a full body massage or just a pep talk before you eat it.

And what are you drinking? Is your tea black, green or white? Your milk soy, almond, coconut, or moo? Do you consume enough water during a single day to water a four acre kale farm? Do you add baking soda and agave to your H2O and drink it ice cold to lose weight or do you just suck it out of the end of a hose in the yard with the dogs?

If you're still cooking with "vegetable" oil, you're a Neanderthal on the foodie evolution chart. The TV docs insist we use sesame seed oil for vitamin E, walnut oil to reduce heart disease, grapeseed oil to lower cholesterol, flaxseed oil for its anti-inflammatory properties, and apricot oil in our hybrid vehicles. I may have gotten that last one wrong because I stopped listening and got a cookie. We're supposed to use all these oils, but we're not supposed to fry anything. I guess you just put some in a glass and shoot it.

The next secret ingredient to good health is seasonings. Cinnamon helps reduce diabetes and is an aphrodisiac. That explains all the people in line at Cinnabon. Tumeric fights infections, cloves relieve digestion, fennel improves your complexion and ginger helps men with re-election (ha!) Chili powder can help with arthritis. As a big fan of hot and spicy myself, I've also found that chili powder can reduce stress by helping you get rid of unwanted guests. All you have to do is sprinkle it liberally in their oatmeal and they'll magically decide a nice hotel would be better for everyone.

Don't forget the supplements: calcium for bones, vitamin D to help bones absorb the calcium, gingko biloba to remember take calcium and vitamin D, raspberry ketone to shrink belly fat, cordyceps mushrooms to increase stamina, nopal cactus to reduce the fatigue brought on by opening all those supplement bottles every morning...

Of course you'll also need to sign up for meditation, acupuncture, quigong, Zumba, spin class, and weight training. Then go out and buy a neti pot, Swedish sauna and some leeches. (Imagine if your grocery list said "neti pot, Swedish sauna and leeches" and you left it behind in your cart at the store! I may just do that.)

I grabbed my calculator and as close as I can figure, eating, drinking, and doing all these healthy things would require 37 hours a day and cost more than a champagne hot air balloon ride over Mars. I think I'll just make like kale and go get a massage and call it good. I feel healthier already.

## Top 5 Valentine's Greetings from the Cat

5. Roses are red, hair balls are hairy, I love you more than I love dairy.
4. All I really need is love, but I wouldn't turn down catnip.
3. You'd be perfect, Valentine, if only you learned to purr.
2. Just because I hide under the bed all day doesn't mean I won't be your Valentine.
1. I only shred your sofa to show my love.


## Top 5 Valentine's Greetings from the Dog

5. How do I love thee? Let me bark the ways.
4. I show my love for you, Valentine, by sitting on your lap until your legs go to sleep.
3. Of all the humans in the world, I'm so happy I chose you to pick up my poo.
2. I will love you unconditionally as long as you feed me cookies.
1. Even if you were a mailman, I'd still want you to be mine.

## I'm a Person, Not a Smudge

Why are there so many creams for women over "a certain age" that have the word "blur" in them? There's Miracle Blur, Opti-Blur, Magic Blur, 5-Second Blur, Victoria's Secret Blur Bra for Boobs Over 50 (okay, I made that last one up, but it's probably on the drawing board).

I don't want to be a blur. I want to be high definition clear. That's right, crows' feet, soft jawline, broadening midsection, dangly boobies and all—I want those in sharp focus. I earned them and I want you to see them, dammit! It's important that when you look at me, you see a 58-year-old woman who has clearly laughed often and well, not a grumpy cat or a Rubik's Cube.

Notice there are no products for men that suggest they become a blur. Their creams firm, lift, harden and other words filled with sexual innuendo. (By the way, do NOT Google euphemisms for erections. Trust me on this!) No, the guys are told that each line and gray hair makes them more distinguished. Sounds like a problem with semantics to me. I think my master's degree and 21 years as a comedy writer and performer makes me look distinguished. But what do I know? I don't write ad copy.

I'm surprised the fashion industry hasn't gotten in on the blurring trend for older women. Imagine the money to be made in selling camo wear to make sure we blend in with our surroundings: sweater sets with Bingo cards on them, velour track suits to match the walls for mall walks, and jeans and t-shirts the color of lumber for those days spent volunteering for Habitat for Humanity. Everyone knows once you reach a certain age, those are the things you spend all your days doing, right?

Or what about a new store called Forever 61 where every item of clothing, every shoe and sock, every accessory was gray and fuzzy… a literal blur? That way younger people could quickly scan a crowd and avoid seeing anyone OLD and LAME. Unless, of course, they were looking for their grandparents in an attempt to make sure they're still in the will.

All of this is moot however, because most people today never look up from their electronic devices. We could all be naked and no one would even notice. Given the choice between naked or blurry, I opt for naked. It's way more fun!

## Enough with Things That Go Boom in the Night

The fireworks stands are up now and I can't wait… to strangle somebody. For the past week, we've had fireworks going off at the schoolyard down the street and it's only the middle of June. If this doesn't stop, I'm going to have to put on my bathrobe, put my hair in curlers, light a cigarette, and go scare me some young men. And you know I'm serious if I'm willing to let a cigarette touch my lips!

Yes, all the other boys are blowing their fingers off too, but that's no reason for you to wake me up at 2:30 a.m. from a dream in which I'm bathing in chocolate as swarthy Greek men who are also mute fan me with magnolia branches. And every time something goes boom, my dogs insist on barking for a full 15 minutes afterward, despite my assuring them that mom will kill the idiots later. Needless to say, I almost woke up on the wrong side of the law this morning. It's not a good sign when immediately after checking my e-mail and Facebook page, I Google "tasers," trying to find out their range. Not far enough if you ask me. I want to be able to do my damage without being seen. I have a reputation as the funny lady on the street - don't want to ruin it with evildoing. Although after a few more sleepless nights, I won't care.

What is the connection between teenage boys (mostly) and their fathers (occasionally) taking to the streets to create a veritable war zone to celebrate our freedoms? Sure, there was firepower involved in becoming the United States of America, but there was also signing of documents, peaceful protesting, sewing of flags, educating of children, surviving the elements, wearing of funny shoes with buckles on them, etc. So why is it that we don't see thread and fabric stands going up every June so that all the children can stitch together their own American flags? I'm sure emergency room docs would much prefer a few finger-pricks than having to sew whole digits back on because kids forget to let go of the bottle rocket.

I love a good 4th of July fireworks display as much as the next person, but one night is enough. And those booms are usually muffled by the sounds of the 1812 Overture or something by Justin Bieber. That I can live with. Especially if I've had a margarita beforehand and it's not 3:30 in the morning.

So boys, take my advice and leave the explosives to the professionals. Or I'm going to have to get my revenge. I'm thinking I'll show up at your house at a time you're sleeping, say 2:00 p.m., and tell graphic jokes about menopause into a bullhorn on your front lawn. You celebrate freedom your way, I'll celebrate mine.

**Keep Your Computers Out of My Closet**

Are you a cyborg? Maybe not yet, but if technology keeps plugging away, you may soon be one—especially if you're a woman. Just take a look at these recent headlines:

- Sony puts Bluetooth technology in a wig.
- Microsoft files patent for a smart bra that evaluates women's moods.
- Solar-powered dress allows women to recharge their own cell phones.

Hey nerdy computer guys: Why are you picking on the women? Where is tie that doubles as a GPS device or the tidy whities that send an app to your cell phone to let you know when the elastic is shot and it's time to buy new ones?

Let me address these ideas one at a time. First, of all—who wears a wig? I mean besides drag queens and clowns. I don't know about you, but when I put a wig on, my head sweats like a menopausal woman at an Arizona dude ranch in August. This can't possibly be good for electronics…not to mention my brain. You see, I have one of those and a lot of scientists have warned me not to put my cell phone too close to it, so the idea of having something sending out signals right on top of my medulla oblongata (is that right, or is that a Queen song?) doesn't seem like a good idea.

Besides, I've never aspired to be a blue-hair (I plan to keep mine orange until the day I dye, uh, die). Now I can add that I don't want to be a Bluetooth hair either.

And a mood bra? Really? According to the article I read, the new technology will measure a woman's heart rate and temperature to determine her emotional state. Why stop there? Why not count the number of chocolate chip cookie crumbs in our cleavage? That's the real key to a woman's mood.

The electronics in the bra then send a message to a cell phone that lets women know when it's not a good time to enter the kitchen or go out to eat with friends. I'm fairly certain they won't stop there, though. There will probably be an app that allows men's cell phones to warn them when the women in their lives are PMSing. Some men just can't seem to figure that out for themselves.

First, I do not want my underwear telling me how I feel. I want to pay someone $150 an hour while I lie on their sofa to do that. And if we're letting women know how they feel, why not invent a ball cap guys can wear that flashes messages to women's cell phones… great guy… Neanderthal… mama's boy? That would be very helpful to me personally.

Second, I have a hard enough time getting through security at the airport because of the damn underwire in my brassiere. How on earth am I going to explain the wires and the red lights flashing (this is how imagine the bra works). "Watch out, it's the bra bomber!" Suddenly women will be required to take off their bras at the TSA station. Calm down, guys, it's probably not going to happen!

And lastly, how would I wash the mood bra? And would that make it happy or depressed?

It seems to me that there has been an unnecessarily large amount of focus of technology on women's boobs. In the past 10 years there have been all kinds of crazy bras. There was the water bra. I tested one of those out the year I started hot flashing. I could have boiled mac & cheese on my chest. That might actually come in handy if I'm out hiking and get lost. Assuming I remember to carry a box of mac & cheese with me at all times.

Then there was the pump-up air bra that let a woman decide how much cleavage to have. This bra was great for playing games on a first date. You could show up with a D cup and if things weren't going well, deflate to an A cup over dessert. I actually have one of these bras. I wear it when I fly over water. Everyone knows your seat cushion won't actually work as a flotation device. Every time I fly over an ocean or lake, I pump my bra up.

If we have a water-landing, I'll be nipples up in the water and everyone will be hanging on to me, like a scene they had to remove from the movie, Titanic.

Finally, we come to the solar-powered dress. I am all for solar power. In fact, I have some panels on my roof that give me free hot water all year round. I might even be willing to wear a dress made of solar panels if I could make my own coffee and avoid the lines at Starbucks. But just to recharge my cell phone? You want to know how that makes me feel? Just ask my bra.

**Resolve This**

It's January, or as it's also known, "Time to hold myself up to some unachievable standards again because I didn't achieve perfection last year. Plus, I ate an entire pumpkin pie last night to clean out the 'fridge, so I need to pay a penance."

Most of us feel pressured to jump on the resolution bandwagon (which usually causes a groin injury) just because everyone else is doing it. We end up with more things on our yearly "To-Do" list than we'll ever be able to accomplish: Lose 30 pounds, run a half marathon, sleep better, vacuum at least once, finish that novel I haven't started, learn all my neighbors' names (not just their dogs' names), stop posting selfies on Facebook, quit making so many lists…"

Part of the problem is that between television, magazines, and the Internet, there is no end to the advice we are given to improve our lives. Last year, for example, we were told that women are supposed to have a space between their thighs when standing up. Really? Why? Are we supposed to be able to keep a cup of coffee warm there or should our children be able to watch the big screen TV when we're standing in front of them?

Some "experts" also decided that there should be a four-inch difference between the circumference of a woman's ankle and her calf, and a seven-inch difference between her calf and thigh. Is the circumference of my thigh pi $r^2$ or 2 x the diameter? Or is it $e=mc^2$? Other than my forgetting geometry, there are a few other problems this rule causes: (a) I don't know where the measuring tape is, (b) I'd have to shave my legs to get an accurate measurement (and it's winter, for heaven's sake), and (c) I really don't care. If worst comes to worse, I'll just start wearing padded tube socks to make up the difference. And maybe get a tattoo of Euclid on my ankle just to be safe.

Men, of course, are supposed to have six-pack abs, which for most is achieved by… well, getting a Sharpie and drawing them on because no amount of ab exercise is going to work for most of the men I know. Hey, if you can buy spray-on-hair, why not a six-pack stencil? Guys are also encouraged to have "guns," biceps so hard they can crack walnuts with them. My male friends have fewer guns and more Nerf slingshots; that's what I love about them.

Some of the suggested health resolutions are truly impossible to achieve. Some health gurus, most of them men, suggest that we have sex at least 200 times a year. Does this mean I'd have to start dating? If so, wouldn't the health benefits of sex (exercise and hormone release) be negated by the stress consequences of dating (anxiety, fear, guilt, sleepy, dopey, and bashful)? Can't I just go to the airport three times a week to get patted down? Security is so thorough now that a first pat-down is like a third date. That should have some health benefits, right?

In addition, we're all supposed to:

- Drink more tea, although deciphering the health benefits of green, black, and white might cause us to grab a Margarita instead (which has lime in it and that IS a fruit);
- Get some sun for the vitamin D, but not so much sun that it makes us look like we're wearing a pleather coat. I guess we all need to carry a stopwatch and time every outing;
- Drink red wine while cutting back on our alcohol intake. Can we also get more sleep while staying up longer and make more friends while spending more time alone reading?
- Wash our hands so frequently that they are chapped so the lotion industry can boost their profits. But we should avoid overuse of antibacterial soaps and products, so I suppose we can wash up with the carbonated beverages we're not supposed to drink anymore;
- Choose real butter and sugar over margarine and artificial sweeteners, but at the same time reduce our fat and sugar consumption because most of us are now classified as "addicts," not just "people who enjoy fat and sugar because it makes us

feel good, especially when we're exhausted from all the other healthy things we've been thinking about doing; and
- Be more grateful while letting our anger out.

Whew, I'm exhausted just thinking about the options. Instead of resolutions this year, I think I'll just choose the first random bumper sticker I see and do whatever it says. I'm hoping for "Visualize whirled peas." I could SO do that.

## Sit, Stay, Remove Your Shoes

In order to get my dogs to do anything I want them to, I have to ask three times. Three seems to be the magic number, unless, of course, they are doing something they really love such as digging up the yard, eating birdseed, or rifling through my guests' coat pockets for tasty treats. Then I can beg, wheedle, whine, and Prancercise about to no avail. The dogs will look at me like they are teenagers who have been asked to turn off their game devices—they recognize my face and are aware that I'm there and have said something, but they don't seem to be able to translate what I've asked of them into a language they understand.

If I'm holding a cookie, I can get their attention faster, but as they are wiener dogs who would get miniature walrus fat if I gave them a cookie every time, I can't rely on treats to do my dirty work. And believe me, they figured out the old bait-and-switch years ago. Dumb, they are not.

I've heard dog trainers and animal behaviorists say that dachshunds are obstinate and oppositional, and that among all the types of animals, they're right up there with spiders in terms of how difficult it is to get them to do anything they'd rather not. I can't debate these opinions, having never tried to train, say weasels or tarantulas, but I can easily think of a group of animals much more difficult to train—humans.

Case in point: I am one of those people who asks everyone who enters my house to remove his or her shoes. I really don't want anyone traipsing dirt, oil, leaves, gum, tar balls, leftover tacos, sequins, ice cream, corners of old love letters, dead dung beetles or whatever else they've got on the soles of their shoes into my house. It's not that I'm a clean freak—all you'd have to do is look at the dishes piled in my kitchen sink to see there is no truth in that assumption. I'm just more comfortable with the dirt my family makes than the dirt others bring in with them. Ick!

Plus, it's easier for strangers not to step on my three small dogs or at least to cause no damage if they're in their stocking feet. So I have legitimate reasons for my request.

Yes, I have also attempted to set up a paw-washing station at my front door for my dogs, but they usually dash inside immediately after an outing, rushing to the kitchen to sit beneath the dog cookie jar waiting for their treat for being good dogs and going outside in the Oregon rain.

In the beginning, as I attempted to train humans to remove their shoes, I was naïve enough to believe that leaving several of mine at the front door would cause guests to ask, "Would you like me to remove mine?" A few did, but the vast majority just barged in, stomping around in their filthy boots, disgusting sneakers, or dangerous stilettos. So I tried the old real estate trick of putting a basket of paper booties by the front door. No one seemed to notice it—perhaps they thought I had gotten a side job as a thoracic surgeon to pay for dog treats?

I truly hated asking each guest to strip down to stocking feet, so I would just grin and bear it when they didn't bare their feet voluntarily. Finally, though, I could no stuff my emotions, so I found a lovely sign online that simply reads, "Please remove your shoes." It's to the point and mounted right next to my front door by the handle everyone must use to get inside. Apparently, however there are further instructions on that sign, invisible to my eye that say: "Please remove your shoes unless you're a contractor, repairman, insurance agent, or ex-husband, or if you arrive with two or more people or are carrying a purse, casserole, or 27 years of emotional baggage." Many folks coming through my door still seem not to be aware of my desires, foot-wise.

I guess I'll have to fall back on dachshund-training techniques. I'm going to attach a Ziploc bag of people cookies to the remove-your-shoes sign and see if that doesn't result in the behavior change I require. If it doesn't work, I'll just hire a TSA agent to give everyone a complete pat down and refuse to let anyone enter without partially disrobing.

## When I Grow Up I Want to Be Betty White

When I was a teenager I thought my grandmother was ancient. She had white hair, wore hand-knit shawls, and kept a bowl of hard candy on her coffee table to distract us from the chocolate she hoarded for herself in the pockets of her apron. We never ate the hard candy because it would have taken a hammer and chisel to get a piece small enough to fit into our mouths. Besides, it was mostly covered in dust and moths.

Grandma was also a germaphobe who Cloroxed everything. We kids were afraid to roll over in bed for fear of ripping the "been bleached so many times there's nothing left but the molecular reminder of" sheets. She insisted our bathwater include a half a cup of bleach (which explains why I'm so pasty). She even drank water out of a Clorox bottle she kept in the refrigerator. Is it any wonder she lived to be 99? Bacteria and fungi didn't stand a chance.

When I was 13, my grandma was 70. I assumed that all women over 60 smelled like rosewater, sat in rocking chairs, bleached their grandchildren, and scolded their husbands to turn up their hearing aids and listen to them nag. Now I know that there are women over 60, 70, and 80 who sport bikinis on the beach (Helen Mirren), make exercise videos (Jane Fonda), and experience a career resurgence powered by Twitter and Facebook (Betty White). I personally know 70 and 80-year-old women who run marathons, teach Tai Chi, do stand-up comedy, and post personal ads online. They may bleach their hair, but they don't bleach their livers.

While in her late 70s, my friend Patrice once showed up for a comedy competition sporting a short spiked fluorescent pink haircut and a t-shirt that spelled out, "I like Ike" in sparkles. She won the competition with her jokes about trying to pick up men with small dogs on Match.com. Patrice once made me spit syrup out my nose when I asked her over brunch why she had a tan in the middle of the long, gray Oregon winter. She explained that she had gotten a spray on-tan to look good on dates. "I thought it was great when I left," she said, "But when I got home and took off my clothes,

I realized that parts of me hang lower than they did in the booth. Parts of me look like Venetian blinds."

Last January, I got invited to judge an ugly holiday sweater contest for a local branch of the Red Hat Ladies. You've got to love a group of women who not only dress to the nines (or the eighteens, for double the fun) whenever they go out, but also procrastinate long enough that their holiday celebrations happen a month later.

The restaurant gave the group a private room, apparently aware of the craziness that ensues when a dozen or so women who no longer let what others think about them dictate their behavior. This room happened to be the one in which the video gaming machines were also located. Three men wandered in during the time we were there, but each got embarrassed by the raucous behavior of women dancing Gangnam style while showing off their sweaters. Nary a guy stayed with us for more than five minutes.

In addition to dirty dancing and dirty jokes, the women told stories about bras and boobs. That's right, boobs. I was laughing so hard that tears ran down my arms, so it's hard to read my notes from that day, but I'll try. One woman said she was flat-chested until her forties, but she wore her older sister's bra when she was young "to keep hay from getting in my shirt." Now there's a sales slogan for brassieres I've never seen: "Farmtex: The bra that keeps the farm out of your clothing."

Another noted that she was born busty. Talk about an image that would have gone viral had there been an Internet in the 1940s. "I was always the most popular girl at barn dances," she bragged, "because the boys said my 'heaters' kept them warm."

Now that I'm closer to 70 than 17, I realize that there is no end to the options that lie ahead (well, except for the option of posing for Swimsuit Illustrated, although I have been lobbying for the midlife and older shoot. I've also been practicing pouting while standing in my underwear on the beach, just in case.)

If I can't be Betty White, I'm going to aspire to become more like an 83-year-old woman I met on a flight to Denver. She was sitting across the aisle and appeared to be a "typical" grandmotherly type, wearing a long floral dress and knitting a baby blanket. When she crossed her legs, however, her dress rode up and exposed a snake tattoo wrapped around her calf and shin. It's great to have such fun role models paving the way for happy, healthy, and totally audacious "golden years." All I need now is a red hat, an audacious tattoo, and a bikini and I'll be ready to face my next three decades in style.

## I Can't See Clearly Now

Whenever the optometrist asks me "What's the smallest line on the chart you can read?" I always shrug and say "Chart? There's a chart?"

I've never been able to see even that giant E, not even when my eyes and I were much younger and skinnier. When I first started being dragged to eye doctors, I thought the whole exam was some kind of intuition test to see if I could figure out the letters by using a sixth sense because I certainly couldn't see (or smell, taste, hear, or feel) them. "I'm picking up something that looks like a... Volkswagen Beetle. Is that right?" It never was.

The first time I remember not being able to see well was in the fourth grade. I used to sit in class and close one eye then the other, comparing how blurry things were with each. If anyone had asked me what I was doing, I'd have lied and answered "demonstrating parallax" because I was just that geeky. (I once dressed Barbie up as Marie Curie and glued some Spanish moss on Ken to transform him into Louis Pasteur for a diorama for school. By the way, they fell in love and had lots of nerdy, bearded babies, despite Barbie Marie's exposure to radiation.)

I became "Four Eyes," (a nickname that followed me into my sophomore year of high school) with my first pair of glasses—black plastic military issue frames, the kind that Clark Kent wore when he was pretending TO NOT BE Superman. These glasses were one of just two options at the Air Force base optical shop: Superman glasses or squinting like a cross-eyed gray wolf. Those same big black glasses are all the rage these days. Zooey Deschanel wears a pair like them on the show New Girl so you know they must be cool (or hot or chill or temperate or whatever temperature-related word means "groovy.") Hipsters wear them too, to seem thoughtful and serious and distract people from the fact that their skinny jeans are way too tight.

But I didn't want hipster Superman glasses. I longed desperately for wire-rimmed frames like John Lennon wore. I thought those glasses would turn me into a rock 'n roll hero. I guess we'll never know.

I've had a few different styles of eyeglasses since my Clark Kent days. There were some cat-eyes in 6th grade. And I can't forget a pair of round tortoise-shell frames that made me look like an overly caffeinated owl. I can't forget because the photos still haunt me from the pages of my middle school and early high school yearbooks. Who-who is that on page 112? I eventually did get wire-rimmed frames, but they made me look too much like John Lennon.

When I was in the 11th grade, I'd had enough and decided it was time for contact lenses. I worked to earn money to pay for them by spray-painting addresses on curbs for my neighbors. It was a job I did with my stepbrother Gary who thought it would "dyn-o-mite" to finish off each address by covering my arms in fluorescent white paint. I earned those first contact lenses the hard way, but they were worth it. I was no longer Four Eyes; I was now Rin-Tin-Grin because of my braces. For some reason, that seemed like trading up.

Two days after I turned 40, as if cued by a wayward gene with a sense of humor, my eye doctor told me I had presbyopia. I said, "That's impossible, I'm Buddhist." Those of you who have to have someone hold a menu up across the street in order to read the specials know the "presbyopia" means "people will now start thinking you're old and forgetful because you will always be patting yourself down looking for reading glasses that are perched on top of your head."

I still wear contact lenses during the day, along with reading glasses that allow me to discern whether the pizza box says to "Cook at 425 degrees for 20 minutes" or "Cool at 735 deciliters for 38 months." At last count, I had seven pairs of reading glasses, all of which occasionally end up on top of my head.

At night, I take out my contacts and wear glasses with progressive lenses because they match my politics. Sorry, I couldn't help myself! Progressive lenses, for those of you who can still focus on the instructions for putting together a bookcase without passing out from the effort, are no-line bifocals. Clark Kent would wear them if he ever aged.

I recently needed a new pair of glasses and started looking for frames that said "She's fun," but couldn't find a store that sold prescription googly-eyed glasses or any with circus stripes. So I got a pair of purple modified cat eye glasses. When I wear them I look cool. Or temperate. Or whatever. Not to mention, I can read the eye chart without channeling my inner psychic!

**That's So Cliché**

Most of the time I am happier than a clam. Of course, I can't say that with 100% certainty because for all I know clams may be partying like it's 1899 in their shells most of the time. But if you look at me and you look at a clam, 9 times out of 10, you're going to say I have the better smile. And really, if you're just trying to attain as much joy as a mollusk, haven't you set your sights just a bit too low? Aspiring to be as happy as a Golden Retriever, on the other hand, now that's a good life goal.

I've always been interested in what the clichés we use say about other creatures and ourselves. Some make perfect sense—"She's got ants in her pants," for example. Having once stood on a fire ant hill while giving someone directions, I know just how unsettling having arthropods in one's knickers can be. As I pranced around trying to shake the buggers off my legs, I believe I may have invented the dance known as "The Sprinkler" that day—that's the one where you grab your foot and hop around in circles.

Some animal clichés, however, leave me scratching my head (and, during flea season, every other part of my body). Take "*naked as a jay bird*," for example. I'll agree that I've never seen a jay dressed in overalls or even a trench coat, but the same is true of most other creatures. Why pick on the jays for public nudity? A better saying, in my opinion, would be "mean as a jaybird." When I lived in Houston, a family of Blue Jays would not allow me into my own yard. Every time I set foot outside, they'd swoop down and attack my head as if they were developing the prototype for Angry Birds. I had to carry a giant golf umbrella just to check the mail or get the newspaper.

When someone drinks too much alcohol for his own good, we'll often say, "*He drinks like a fish.*" I see how the puckering of fish lips could look like they're drinking, but personally, I think fish look more like they're kissing than knocking back a six-pack of beer, so why not "He kisses like a fish"? The best part of this cliché would be that no one would know whether it's a compliment.

"*Does the cat have your tongue?*" If so, why were you sticking it out? I grew up with several cats and have taken care of dozens of felines when their people have gone on vacation. Not one has ever gone for my tongue— my feet, hair, hands, neck, stomach, and liver, yes. Perhaps my breath is not appealing to felines. If someone is having trouble coming up with the right words for the situation, why don't we say, "She's as quiet as a jellyfish" instead? Or "Shellfish caused your tongue to swell up?" Or we could leave the animals out of it altogether and try, "What's the matter, has peanut butter glued your tongue to the roof of your mouth?"

When the person in front of you at the grocery store is talking on her cell phone so loudly that even people in the parking lot can hear her describe how cold her doctor's hands were during her last annual exam, *doesn't that just get your goat*? If so, should you really have a goat in the store? Is it a helper goat of some kind? When we get annoyed or angry we often bring up ruminants, but always goats, never camels, alpacas or pronghorns. I'm going to start saying, "Doesn't that just get your pronghorn" to see if it catches on. When we're annoyed, it would make more sense to say "Doesn't that just make you want to butt heads with someone?" Or even, "I'm so irritated that I could eat tin cans and the bumper off a 1962 Chevy Nova."

While we're on the subject of being irritable, let's discuss the phrase "*mad as a wet hen.*" I've never had the opportunity to shower with a chicken, although it is on my bucket list. It makes sense, however, that hens would not enjoy running through the sprinkler or playing on the Slip 'n Slide, but then most animals that roam the earth and air probably prefer being dry. Just look at a squirrel in a rainstorm. Why don't we say "mad as a wet squirrel"? Better yet, "mad as a wet woman who has just had her hair done and is one her way to her sister's wedding in a $500 bridesmaids' dress she'll never be able to wear anywhere else, especially now because it is dry clean only." Now that's catchy!

If I had more time, we could delve into how "*as a crow flies*" isn't as straight a line as we think because crows spend all their time heckling larger birds, how "*working like a dog*" must involve testing sofas and mattresses, and how if "*the world is your oyster,*" you probably need to bathe more. But I have to work like a dog, kiss a few fish to see whether they're good at it, and look for my goat. I hear someone got him. And that just gets my pronghorn!

## Give Me a Shower Any Day

I rarely take a bath. I usually prefer a five-minute shower – it not only saves water, there's far less chance of any part of my body becoming pruney. Next to pasty and "cellulitey," pruny is my least favorite look, and it's the one I have some control over.

But once in a while when you've had one of those days, you long for a nice hot bath surrounded by candles and softly playing oldies music (or softly playing hip hop music if you find that more relaxing). Yesterday was one of those days. It started with a 6:30 a.m. phone caller who insisted she had reached her doctor's office and I needed to make an appointment for her, was quickly followed by the discovery that my roof was leaking (again), and was punctuated by my trying to un-jam a sheet of paper from my printer and catching my hair in the fax machine in the process. There is not a button on my machine to fix that kind of problem. I looked.

Clearly what I needed was a bath, because a tubful of water is less expensive than mood-enhancing drugs or a therapist. And I was all out of bubble wrap. I immediately gathered together all the candles I could find in the house and marched into the bathroom with them. I've learned enough about bathing by candlelight (mostly from soap operas) to know that for a relaxing bath, the best scents are lavender or ylang-ylang, but I had to make do with what we had around the house: a cinnamon apple votive, a goat's milk pillar, and the nubs of two pumpkin-pie scent tapers left over from Thanksgiving. Suddenly I was stressed and hungry.

Because my tub isn't one of those garden tubs with a wide ledge on which you can grow plants and cool freshly-baked pies, I put my candles on the back of the toilet tank and lit them. Then I ran the bathwater. So far, so good. I looked under the sink for bubble bath, but the closest I came was toilet cleanser, so I headed into the kitchen for the dishwashing detergent. It promised to make me smell like a mountain spring and leave no greasy residue. Good enough for me.

Finally, I lowered myself into the tub. Aaah. The water temperature was perfect. I closed my eyes and visualized myself at a health spa deep in the desert Southwest, where the roofs never leak. I took a few deep cleansing breaths. It smelled like "think outside the box" day at a candle factory, but I was committed to the fantasy. I could hear the sounds of my imaginary massage therapist preparing my hot stone massage in the room next door. And the personal nutritionist preparing my four-course healthy lunch in the kitchen. What can I say, I have an active imagination. It helps make up for my inactive bank balance.

Suddenly I smelled something new. Something kind of woodsy. I opened my eyes slightly to find that the hand towel hanging next to toilet had caught fire. In a flash, I jumped up out of the tub and tossed it into the bath water. Unfortunately, as I flung the flaming towel into the tub, it ignited the shower curtain and a red-hot hole started melting its way through the plastic. Can I say that melting shower curtain is NOT a relaxing scent? And the mellow sounds of James Taylor's crooning were suddenly drowned out by the screech of my hallway smoke detector. Which, of course, was followed by the barking of my dogs (they hate the smoke alarm noise as much as I hate being pruny).

I reassured the canines we would all be okay as I yanked the shower curtain off the rod and stuffed it in the tub. This maneuver extinguished the fire, but it also ripped the curtain rod out of the wall. Bits of sheet rock filled the air, but I didn't have time to worry about the damage because I was running down the hall to grab the smoke detector and put an end to ear-splitting wail. As I stood naked except for a few not-strategically-placed dishwashing liquid bubbles, waving the smoke detector back and forth near an open window, my next-door neighbor walked by. He pretended not to notice, but I know better. Guess who's going to be the talk of the cul-de-sac this month? Again.

I headed back to the bathroom to survey the damage. If they want to invent a candle that best captures the aroma of the moment, they would probably call it "Suspected Arson." The toilet seat was covered with candle wax and sheetrock dust. The tub was filled with semi-burnt bathroom accessories. And the candles had blackened the wall and the underside of the medicine chest.

Here's what I'm thinking. The next time I'm in the mood for a nice relaxing bath, I'm going to remember this day and instead take a nice long shower by flashlight instead. It's bound to be less stressful.

**Not My Type**

I just got a new cellphone [insert festive sound effects here]. I don't know if you know this, but if you leave your phone under running water for more than a minute, it may go all wonky on you. (Side note: If you're in a public bathroom all alone and you hear what sounds like water even though you're not washing anything, there's a 98% likelihood that your purse or backpack has set off the auto-faucet and water is pouring over your phone, wallet, business cards, a handful of expired coupons, samples of dog hair you have in a manila envelope for a reason you care not to share with anyone, and a note to yourself to remember to stop being so klutzy… And no, holding your cell phone under the automatic hand dryer will not fix it. Neither, in my case, will putting it in a bag full of rice overnight. I used instant rice; that may have been the problem. Perhaps had I taken my phone out after 5 minutes, it would have been done.)

The good news is that my old cell phone only had five contacts in it and I know all those numbers by heart because my head is not cluttered up with unnecessary information such as where I've parked and whether I've taken my vitamins.

The other good news is now I have a brand spanking new cell phone that I can talk to. I say things such as, "Find a cheap Italian restaurant." When I do, however, it just lies in my hand  morosely, occasionally rolling its eyes and mumbling, "Whatever." You see, I did NOT get a smart phone. My phone company representative could barely repress her laughter when I called from my landline (yes, I have a landline!) and asked which phones had the lowest IQ or tended to be kept late in class for throwing spitballs or cracking wise. These are the kinds of phones I get along with best.

The fact is, I don't want to always be connected to the Internet. I have a hard enough time getting any work done on my computer knowing that Facebook and e-mail are just a click away, waiting to show me new kittens who misuse grammar and puppies teaching other puppies to use the stairs. When I'm out of my office, I prefer to sit through a conversation with a

Don't Laugh! You'll Wake the Dog

friend or stranger without feeling my thigh vibrate every time someone sends a text offering me mail-order brides or free money from far-off princes. Call me crazy – you won't be the first.

Many people wonder how anyone can survive without the necessary to constantly write scathing Yelp reviews does while stuck in line at the DMV or waiting in a doctor's office. I can't speak for everyone, but I'll tell you what I do: I think. I look around. I chat. I hear stuff and not just the voices in my head. I practice Kegel exercises. I memorize people's phone numbers because I know that I operate just fine when soaking wet.

So my new phone isn't very intelligent, but it does have a Qwerty keyboard. I like that because it reminds me of old times. You see, I learned to type in 1972 on an old metal Underwood typewriter. You had to press the keys with the force of a jackhammer to get them to strike the inky ribbon and place a single letter on a page of paper, but I got good at it. In fact, forgive me for bragging here, I was on the regional typing team in the 11th grade. Typing was my Plan B in case becoming president/ballerina/astrophysicist didn't work out.

I worked as a secretary while putting myself through college and graduate school, so those typing skills came in handy. In the early 80s, the business world was blown away by the IBM Correcting Selectric, a typewriter that allowed you to back up and type over your mistakes, as long as you caught your error before moving on to the next word. Sales of Wite-Out, and the contact high it created in regular users, plummeted. In 1982, my first ex-husband built our first personal computer with supplies from Radio Shack. It was a clunky box with a flashing green cursor that looked like something out of science fiction move, but I typed on it like a madwoman, drunk with pleasure from the knowledge that any mistakes I made could be corrected at any time, even after I'd turned off the machine and rebooted it. Would wonders never cease? You can imagine how I felt when word processing was born! Cut and paste? Be still my heart!
So now I have a tiny little keyboard on my very own cell phone. All I need to do is figure out how to get all ten of my fingers on those miniature keys

while holding a magnifying glass in my teeth so that I can see them. Watch out world, I may just text my next column.

**New Year's Dachs-solutions**

As far as I know, dogs don't make New Year's resolutions – unless "Hound mom for another cookie" counts.

But when it comes to living life well and being the best person-who-is-probably--60%-canine-given-the-amount-of-dog-hair-on-my-clothes, I don't turn to health experts, fitness coaches, spiritual gurus, or the cast of Frozen for advice. I turn to my wiener dogs. And because they're so smart, I've decided to share some of their wisdom with you as you contemplate how to make 2015 your best year ever.

1.    **Keep your expectations low**. My dachshunds are only 2" off the ground, so it makes sense that they set the bar lower than, say, Golden Retrievers or stilt walkers. Compare this with some humans I know who expect perfection from themselves and everyone else. Life is much more fun when you enjoy the pleasures – and the snacks – within your reach.

2.    **Dream outrageously.** You can find happiness in small things like a tennis ball that hasn't already been pre-soaked by a slobbery sibling and still dream big. When you fall asleep, if you don't kick and whimper and drool a little, chances are you need more audacity in your imaginary life. Make up your own stories about how you scaled the Douglas Fir tree in the back yard to chase the squirrel and the day the garbage collector brought you trash instead of taking it away.

3.    **Be as disobedient as your looks will allow**. When it comes to great personality traits, disobedience is highly underrated, except to doxies who are proud to point to the fact that they make almost every list of dogs most difficult to train. Obedience means doing what others want you to when they want you to... and really, where's the fun in that? Who wants to sit and stay when there is so much fun to be had? That vegan gluten-free cupcake on the coffee table isn't getting eaten by the most obedient dog in the house, now is it?

4.    **Practice looking innocent**. If you're going to get away with high levels of disobedience, there will be times you'll have to pretend you know nothing about the half-eaten sock hanging from your mouth or the piddle on the rug in the hall. The most convincing "I didn't do it" look is nose down, eyes up. If you can add a tiny whimper, followed by a sigh, not only will you NOT be in trouble, you'll probably get a reward. Can you say ice cream? And if your human decides to post a "dog-shaming" picture of you on Facebook, you can milk her guilt at doing so for a year of free rides to the park.

5.    **Clown around every day**. If you're not doing something goofy for the sheer pleasure of being silly, you're missing out on big dog fun. Tossing a stuffed animal in the air over and over again will not only bring a smile to everyone's face, it's also great exercise on a rainy afternoon. So is chasing your tail rolling on your back as if you're making carpet angels. At the very least, practice wacky and dopey looks every day until everyone around you cracks up.

6.    **Set your own schedule**. Daylight savings time is for humans… and cats. If you're hungry at 4 a.m., it's time to eat! Just make sure to cut back a little during your five other daily meals. After all, you want to save room for any treats that may be coming your way unexpectedly.

7.    **When you're happy, wiggle your entire body.** Some folks think they're happy, but they never notify their faces. Dachshunds show joy from nose to tail. Penny, my smallest, somehow manages to levitate, with all four feet off the floor with sheer ebullience. Forget typing LOL or smiling and nodding; try shaking your entire body from head to toes. Sure, some folks will think you're crazy, but crazy is better than sad and moody.

8.    **If you're going to bark, bark loudly.** No point in whispering; if you have something to say, make sure you're heard above the TV or the sounds of your human pretending she is Lady Gaga. If it's important to you, don't

keep it bottled up inside. Silence is for de-squeaked stuffed animals. The bark will set you free.

9.   **Shake it off.** Whenever life rains on your parade, shake, shake, shake until everything is back in place. Then walk away like nothing happened.

10.   **Show your love irrationally**. Lie across your loved one's feet so she can't leave the house. Stand on his chest while he exercises and smother him with kisses until he stops and plays with you. Snuggle up next to her, with your siblings on the other side, so there's no way she can get up in the middle of the night to get a snack without you knowing about it. Wag your tail so hard it leaves welts on his legs. Or do it your own way, you disobedient human, you.

Of course, when it comes to New Year's resolutions, you could just vow to eat less, exercise more, and spend less time on Facebook. But the dachshunds don't

**Summer Separates the Boys from the Girls**

I was at a garage sale one afternoon last weekend when a man in his eighties noticed a very large weed wacker near the door.

"That for sale?" he asked as he rushed over to it as fast as his cane would let him.

"Yep. We're asking $5," the woman answered with that *I hope he's not just toying with me* tone that every garage sale organizer gets as the day wears on and it becomes clear than all that stuff, including the treadmill and the giant moose with blue eye shadow, is going to have to be packed up and dragged inside again.

"Sold," the man said under his breath, hoping to transact the deal before his wife noticed. No such luck. A curly-haired sprite of a woman left the Jane Fonda videotapes she'd been perusing and appeared at his side in a flash, her tiny fists balled up on her hips.

"Bob, you can't even lift that thing. Besides, we don't have weeds in our apartment."

"I know, Bonnie. But it's got three horses. Three! For $5. That's a steal."

Later that same day, I was at the mall with a friend when I overheard two women in the dressing room talking.

"I read that Jennifer Hudson went from a size 16 to a 6. If she can do that, I bet by July 4th weekend I'll be skinny enough to get into this size 12 sundress! Only fifteen more pounds and I'm so there!"

"Me too! Look out world; soon there will be less of us to love!"

To me, these stories capture how men and women's experiences of summer differ: for the guys it's all about bigger, faster, and louder, while most women try to become smaller and less conspicuous. It's Godzilla versus The Shrinking Woman.

Here's another case in point: while walking my dogs recently, a man waved to us from atop his riding lawnmower. He said something too, but the roar of the suburban tractor drowned it out. Perhaps what he said was "I know my lawn is only the size of a postage stamp and I have to back this mower into the street to turn it around, but I AM KING OF THE WORLD!"

I can see how a riding lawn mower would be a great idea for someone with several acres of grass, but I can't for the life of me think of why guys need one to trim the two dandelions that have sprouted in the driveway cracks. I have more carpet than he has lawn, yet I have never lain awake at night wishing someone would invent a riding vacuum cleaner with an onboard chocolate dispenser. Of course, the testosterone coursing through my veins wouldn't fill up a pink Hello Kitty thimble, so what do I know?

Speaking of bigger and louder, that definitely applies to fireworks. Don't get me wrong – I love a beautiful fireworks show, with each explosion timed to the 1812 Overture or Lady Gaga's Poker. But the guys can never get enough of things that go boom in the night. I once had a neighbor who stuck leftover firecrackers under his weeds in an attempt to blow them sky high. He was happy with the result too, despite the fact that he ended up singeing off most of his eyebrows. Most women are happy to settle for pretty – and quiet – sparklers and leave our eyebrow maintenance to the professionals.

Of course, women's summertime pursuit of trying to achieve the impossible is just as dangerous. I'm totally onboard with staying fit and healthy, but most of us can do that in the average-sized body we're meant to have. My personal feeling is that zero is an imaginary number and if you diet and exercise your way there, you'll disappear. I like there to be enough of me to cause a commotion or at least hold up my sparkler.

While the guys are blowing things up and marveling at how much horsepower their new riding BBQ has (laugh now, but you know it's only a matter of time), many women are turning down potato salad and popsicles because they have too many calories, and don't even get us started on the trans fats!

Women would do well to take a page from the guys' handbook (they're not reading it anyway, because as well all know, men don't need instructions). Let's spend more time this summer focusing on all the power we have under our hood and not on the size of our chassis. Now that's a goal worth pursuing this summer!

## Wii? Oui!

I've been working out a lot lately. Or, to be more precise, working in… my living room to be exact. To anyone passing by my window, it may appear that I'm repeatedly swatting at imaginary insects, but I'm actually working my way up the virtual tennis rankings. I'm now tennis pro, but only on carpet.

I'm also an expert bowler, semi-accomplished volleyball and soccer player, and I could knock someone out cold if I had to, thanks to my boxing training. It's a real boost to my self-esteem, especially for someone who flunked tennis twice, once bowled a 7, and is not ashamed to say that when a ball comes flying at my head, my first instinct is to run in the opposite direction.

The best part of working out with Wii is that he (I prefer to think of him as a French man named "Oui") is convinced that I'm somewhere between 31 and 37 years old. And no, I don't work out by candlelight and pour wine onto the console.

I don't typically play videogames, primarily because Pac Man scared me in the 80s. But a few months ago I decided I needed to add some fitness equipment to my home gym – I already have a 5-lb. hula hoop, a Pilate's ball, and 76-lbs. worth of dachshunds who unlike kettle bells wriggle when you pick them up. I considered a treadmill or an elliptical machine, but both are heavy and hard to drag out to a garage sale. So I chose something lightweight and portable. That's when I said oui to Wii.

If you're not familiar with Wii's virtual workouts, let me answer a few quick questions for you:

- Can you really get a workout with a video game? Yes, indeed, you can. After six weeks of hitting fake tennis balls and spiking imaginary volleyballs, I can see muscles on my body again. Of course, I have to put my reading glasses on to do so, but I know they're there.

- How much room do you need to work out? It depends on how physically demonstrative you are. I'm a mover and a shaker (the latter is one of the reasons I decided to up my exercise program) and have on occasion knocked over furniture while shooting virtual hoops or slalom skiing. My friend Marcy, on the other hand, used to soundly beat me at tennis while sitting on her sofa nursing her baby. She could probably still do so, but her son is eating real-people food now.
- How does the program decide how fit you are? The balance board weighs you and calculates both your body mass and "age" prior to each workout. Fortunately, you are allowed to subtract out the weight of your clothing, but when I claimed my outfit weighed 50 lbs., Oui laughed and laughed. It was a haughty French laugh and it shamed me into choosing a more reasonable 3 lbs. instead. On days I've snacked too much, I work out in a backless paper hospital gown.
- How do you stay motivated to work out regularly? I have three different Wii exercise programs and two of them include personal trainers who give helpful advice such as "My grandma can hit harder" and "Do you stumble when you walk?" Part of me really wants to prove them wrong. There's also lots of positive feedback; my favorites include: "You're in control of this exercise," "With dancing like that, you must be the life of the party," and "Care for a glass of Chablis, mon ami?" Okay, perhaps I've imagined that last one, but hey, it's my virtual world.

As with anything, there are some things to watch out for when working out with Wii. First, you may find yourself talking to your television set even more than during reality shows. For example, if you don't hold the remote exactly right, a squat or a bicep curl may not get counted, which can be quite frustrating. I usually end up chiding Oui, "I just did that squat. If you'd pay closer attention to me and not to those seagulls flying by, you'd know that!"

You may also develop a virtual form of schizophrenia if you play too much tennis. Wii tennis games are doubles matches and your team consists of you... and you. I frequently find myself fuming, "That ball was on your side of the court! Come on, help me out here!" It doesn't occur to me until the game is over that I've been yelling at myself.

And I'm sure that if you start to believe you're actually as good a real sports as you are a Wii sports, you will get a rude awakening when you step on a court, alley, field, track, or gym. On the plus side, anyone watching will probably get a good belly laugh.

I must go now. I have a tennis date with Oui. I

## Spiders and Swimsuits, Oh My!

Ah, summer and a young middle-aged girl's fancy turn to... new garage doors! Forget summer vacation -- for me sturdy steel doors for my garage are the pinnacle of the high life. Plus, I don't have to wear a swimsuit to use them! Now that's what I call a bonus.

My old garage doors came with the house when it was built in 1965. This was confirmed by the guy who gave me the estimate for installation of new doors. "Yep, we installed these things fifty years ago," he said. I told him that was way before my time and giggled like a sixth-grader. He seemed to accept my youthful status. I could barely restrain myself from kissing him full throttle (it helped to think that it would probably add $100 or so to my bill.) He would not, however, confirm my suspicion that the original doors were made of cardboard and spiders.

The old doors long ago lost their bottom seal (as have many of my friends). I jest. A bottom seal is that rubber doohickey that runs along the bottom of the door to keep out debris. This explains why I've raked more leaves out of the garage than I have the yard. It may also explain why I often find the neighbor's cat curled up in my anti-gravity chair reading through my old tax records.

Like many people – perhaps women people and the obsessive compulsives more than most – I felt compelled to clean the garage before the installer arrived. This is not something I do frequently because truth be known, it scares me. The garage, not cleaning. Okay, both. While the rest of my house is like my conscious mind – colorful, quirky, and mostly neat – my garage is more like my subconscious. It's dark and dirty, and I'm afraid if I root around too much, I'll find boxes filled with repressed childhood memories or scary clowns, or in the case of my childhood, both.

I usually only go in the garage to back out my car and as I do, I metaphorically wave some burning sage to keep away the evil spirits. The only people in my house who aren't freaked out by what's out there are my dachshunds—any dog who will chase a badger down a hole isn't going to be scared away by a few shadows and some giant shoes.

Personally, I think that "Garage Therapist" would be a great occupation for someone. He or she could lead you through the 5 stages of garage grief – denial that the garage even exists, anger at yourself for letting it get to the state it's in, bargaining (which is the reason there are so many boxes from online retailers stored out there), repression of bad memories (such as when my ex-husband filled the garage from floor to ceiling with Hot Wheels cars for five years), and "exceptance" (making an exception to clean up this once because you refuse to let someone see how messy your space and your psyche are).

I opened the one old garage door that works at the push of a button and the other which works at the push, shove, grunt, howl, and curse of deadlifting 70 or so pounds. In the light of day, the place isn't quite as spooky. While sweeping out dirt, leaves, and memories, I did a quick inventory of what was out "there": bicycle, dog stroller, dog wagon, old dog ramps, leftover carpet from dog ramps, an anti-gravity chair I don't use because it's impossible to sit in with three dogs (do you sense a theme?), wooden ladder which used to belong to my second ex-husband's father (ah, memories), toolbox filled with all the tools I should be banned from using, a large storage shelf filled with comedy props and holiday items, recycling bins, a wet vac, and everything that I don't want to put in a landfill but am too forgetful to remember to take to the appropriate location for recycling (CFL bulbs, batteries, screen door, busted rain barrel, former mother-in-law...). Oh, and approximately 16,739 spiders, give or take a few.

The garage door installer came today. He was a tall red-headed young man who listened to country music and worked right through lunch. He didn't seem overly impressed by my efforts at making sure he had a clean space in which to work, but I pretended he was grateful.

And now I have brand-spanking new steel garage doors that are blissfully easy to open and close (even the one that doesn't work at the push of a button). They're insulated and quiet and each have a lovely bottom seal. They make me want to be a better person. Maybe I'll finally get around to organizing my stuff. And you know what? I may put on some Jimmy Buffet tunes and wear a swimsuit to do it! After all, it IS summer!

## Egging Me On

I love the morning melodies of chickens roaming free in the backyards of my neighbors. They sound chatty and happy like nerdy girls on the bus on the first day of school. As I walk by with my dogs, I imagine they've got their Texas Instruments calculators out to determine whose eggs have the biggest circumference. (Yes, in my mind these chickens use technology from the 80s. They also have big hair and shoulder pads.)

Several families in a two-block radius of my house raise little cluckers. For a while, there was a house one block over with chicks who free-ranged in the middle of the street, which made dog-walking quite an adventure. (Note to grammar nerds, of which I am one: I choose to use "who" for chickens; I reserve "that" for inanimate objects, such as my ex-husband.) Who needs video games when dragging three wiener dogs down a fowl-filled street provides more entertainment AND exercise to boot? By the way, if you're a game developer and want to create this game, I'd like credit and I'd like it to be called "Doxies Coming Home to Roost." Thank you.

I once got to watch a friend's chicks hatch in an incubator. That was the day I realized that no matter how hard I worked at anything, I could never equal the energy and stamina it takes just to get out of an egg and into the world. I pulled a muscle just thinking about it now.

The truth is that I'd love to have my own chickens to wake up to, but I'm hen-pecked enough by three dachshunds, four koi (one the size of a Volkswagen Beetle), flocks of hungry wild birds, and 17 squirrels who are brazen enough to come to the back door to complain when I've fallen behind on their feeding schedule. I've named them all Ralph, so I don't have to try to tell them apart. It was either that or make them little name tags, which they refused to wear, claiming the adhesive backing was itchy.

So rather than adding to my menagerie, I get my hen fix by providing part-time chicken sitting services when my neighbors have to go out of town. It's the only sitting job I've ever had for where the charges pay me themselves—in freshly laid eggs. I just have to remember not to take home the fake eggs that are meant to encourage the girls. These make lousy midday snacks.

My love of neighborly chickens has grown now that I'm vegan except for eggs from hens I know personally. I'm happy that my neighbors can keep my supplied--especially in summer when I must devote 24 hours a day making zucchini bread to keep my house from being featured on the front page of this newspaper under the headline: "Suburban Dwelling Swallowed by Marauding Zucchini Plant."

For those of you who don't personally know fowl of the two-legged kind, they come in many varieties. There are Black-Tailed Japanese Bantams (which may or may not also be a weight class for boxers), Plymouth Rocks (who should wear little buckled shoes, but don't), Silver Penciled Wyandottes (a great country band name, right?), Buff Orringtons (I imagine they work out every afternoon with kettle bells and heavy weights), Silver Spangled Hamburgs (the best accessorizers), and Foghorn Leghorns. I say, I say, that last one was a joke, son.

Not being a chicken expert myself, I'm not sure what the specific differences in varieties are—whether Bantams are better layers or Orringtons can carry a tune, for example. From my personal experience as a chicken sitter, I can tell you, however, that the blondes, whatever kind they are, tend to be overly protective of their food and the brunettes gather in a corner and complain about how hungry they are. The reds? Well, they hide in the shade reading Christopher Moore novels. Oh, wait, that's me.

The next time you take a walk around your neighborhood, keep your ears pealed for the sounds of satisfied chickens in nearby back yards. And if you too want to add fowl to your flora and fauna, you know where you can find a good sitter.

## What's to Eat?

Four girlfriends and I recently rented a house on the Oregon coast with our five dogs (my three and two "cousins"). We did not throw drinks in each other's faces, toss furniture across the room, or try to vote each other out of the cottage… which is why we won't ever have our own reality show. People would fall asleep immediately.

We did laugh; play games; walk on the beach; complain about our mothers, boyfriends, husbands, ex-husbands, and hot flashes; and eat. And eat. And… well… eat.

In many parts of the country, serving meals for five women isn't a big deal, but things are different when those five women all hail from Eugene. In our group we had: one vegetarian, one vegan, one omnivore who loves anything that will sit still long enough for her to bite it, one woman on Weight Watchers, and one lactose/gluten/sugar-free/free-range/locally grown/is there anything leftian.

We had daily conversations such as this:

Woman 1: Whose grapes are these in the crisper?

Woman 2: They're anyone's. Feel free to have some.

Woman 1: Are they free range, organic, no-spray, locally grown grapes that were told they were beautiful from childhood and raised to the sounds of classical music? Or are they covered with toxic chemicals and picked by underpaid, overworked immigrant workers who are just trying to support their families? Because if they're the latter, my karma won't allow me to even be in the same room with them.

Woman 2: I forget. But I washed them in soapy water.

Woman 1: No thanks. I'll have some soy ice cream with hemp sprinkles instead.

During my earlier years in Texas, people like us were known as "finicky" eaters. We were frowned upon and pressured by friends and family to, "*At least try some of the barbecued fish because fish is really more a vegetable than an animal.*" Uh-huh. And beer is really just thinner milk with a kick. I remember once cooking up a pot of vegetarian chili – which had raisins and cashews in it – for a chili cook-off in Houston. People avoided my booth like I was a feminist liberal who protested rodeos (which I was, but I didn't itemize those "sins" on the ingredient list for my chili.)

It used to be difficult to find recipes to meet the needs and wants of guests with dietary restrictions, but these days there are dozens of cooking shows on television catering to everyone from those who enjoy deep fat-frying everything including their oven mitts to those who consider a single glazed carrot with a dollop of wild ginger cardamom pear compote to be a complete meal. You can also Google recipes for any dish. I typed in the words "gluten-free" and got 55 million hits. Of course, probably 54 million of those are actually ads for gluten-free Viagra, but those first million are probably legit.

Even with all the help available on television and online, most of our cooking habits are formed in early childhood. Unfortunately, when it came to preparing meals, my family followed the motto, "*If you can't be a good example, be a horrible warning.*" The only meals I remember my mom and two stepmoms making were fish sticks and Tater Tots, and fried pork chops with pineapple slices. My dad made two memorable dishes—kidney beans with elbow macaroni and sugar, and tuna fish with mayo and sugar. Is it any wonder I can eat my way through a dessert bar faster than you can say, "Do you really need another slice of raspberry cheesecake?"

When we were "between mothers," we had a Czechoslovakian housekeeper named Ricki who considered peanut butter a condiment to be used with every meal. Perhaps this was less a culinary decision than a way to try to get the four of us kids to stop yammering for a few minutes every day.

Once I got married, I hoped that I would pick up better cooking skills from my mothers-in-law, but not so much. MIL #1 was considered a great cook, perhaps because she used bacon fat in almost everything, even her famous pecan pies. Her primary contribution to my food education was to pass on a copy of an original Betty Crocker cookbook, which I still have to this day. Three quarters of the book – the pages called "Main Dishes," all of which involve meat – is in pristine condition. The pages of the dessert section have been drooled on a few too many times.

MIL #2 made great Rice Krispies bars, but that was a recipe I had already picked up from Ms. Crocker before I married her son. MIL #3 was 82 when we met and wasn't interested in cooking anything for anyone (and who could blame her?)

Fortunately, given my creative bent and my willingness to break any rule, I've moved forward from the unfortunate cooking habits I grew up with. I have two culinary secrets: (1) I always substitute at least three things in every recipe. For example, let's say a recipe for Carrot Cilantro Soup includes olive oil, onions, coriander seeds, carrots, vegetable stock, and cilantro. I'll use, for example, olive oil, onions, flax seeds, sweet potatoes, vegetable stock, and chili pepper. Voila, Spicy Sweet Potato Flax Soup! (2) I don't include sugar in any of my entrees because I have to save room for dessert.

I'm happy to say – and at least three people who have eaten my cooking will support me on this – by using these two rules, I can whip up passably edible dishes. Even the pickiest eater will enjoy the lovely aroma of my food, even if she won't eat it.

**I Am a Craftoholic, Please Help Me!**

I should not be allowed in craft stores. My picture should be posted at the registers and professional craft store bouncers should escort me out before I'm allowed to spend any of my hard-earned money. Even if I do have a half-price coupon.

The fact is, despite having logged dozens of hours of TV time watching people hot glue, string beads, decoupage, and make their own paper, my sum total of craft talent could fit in a thimble. Which is a good place for it because given my lack of sewing skills, I won't be needing a thimble for any other purpose.

Unfortunately, I am a craftoholic. Which is an immense problem throughout the months of November and December, known in crafting circles as "Of course you have time to make your own wrapping paper and homemade gifts, just stop exercising and going to work, and perhaps going to the bathroom." I LOVE craft stuff. Rubber stamps and glitter and doll eyes that follow you from room to room and velvet ribbons and iron-on transfers that say cute things such as "Happy Howlidays." When I see an ad in the Sunday paper for scrapbooking supplies or 600-piece oil paint kits, I somehow end up in my car, drawn to the crafts store like there's a giant magnet under my hood and I am powerless to control where I go.

It doesn't help that I have friends who can create Victorian lamps in their sleep or knit afghans while riding a Harley to their next holiday party. They – along with the perky do-it-yourself TV hosts – are so persuasive at convincing me that I too can be a crafty girl. Despite decades of evidence to the contrary.

I offer as proof: the time I tried to create a mosaic tile planter and ended up with a ceramic pot with squiggly grout lines on its sides and tiles piled up around the bottom, like some kind of tutu. Even the squirrels, notorious for using my planters as places to store their winter nut supplies, wouldn't come anywhere near the thing. And the guy at the thrift store looked at me funny when I donated it.

Then there was the time I decided to hand-paint a table I'd found at a garage sale to look like one of those expensive tables with folk art and cute sayings around the edges such as "Always look on the bright side," "Friends ARE family," and "This table cost more than my health insurance premium." I forgot temporarily that my handwriting is often mistaken for a drunken doctor's. What was supposed to be one of my favorite quotes from my favorite philosopher Jimmy Buffet, "If we couldn't laugh, we'd all go insane," turned out looking more like an orange and purple trail of slug slime. I offer my guests money to guess what it says. So far, I haven't lost a cent.

Last, but not least, I once hand-sewed a pillow not only to my jeans, but in three places, to my leg. One would imagine the pain would have stopped me from repeating the mistake, but I was so entranced by the woman on television encouraging me not to stop at pillows, but to go ahead and reupholster my furniture too, that I was completely oblivious. For all I know, my socks could have been on fire too. But that only happens when I use a hot glue gun.

Sadly, there is no twelve-step program for those of us who have drawers full of yarn that back when we bought it in the 90s was going to become a fringed poncho for a friend. No group therapy for we who believe we can learn to screen print our own t-shirts if only we order the machine on that late-night infomercial. No rehab for those of us who have shown up at work with our thumb and index finger not only glued together, but with green and yellow glitter seemingly permanently affixed to them.

I write this to ask for your help. The next time you see a friend or a stranger standing in a craft store with fabric paint under her fingernails and pom-pom critters in her hair staring at doll parts or beading supplies and mumbling to herself, "This time I know I can do it," gently pat her hand and walk her out the front door. Do NOT suggest she try an easier project. Even something as innocent-sounding as making snowmen out of pipe cleaners can be a gateway drug for those of us with this addiction. Instead, point her towards the nearest mall and in your most soothing voice say, "Things are already put together for you over there." It's the best holiday gift you can give someone like me.

Ooh, look, an ad for half-price candle-making supplies!

## It's (Not) a Date!

It's been more than ten years since I've been on an official date (as certified by the Office of Dating and Other Excruciatingly Uncomfortable Social Experiences).

Don't get me wrong, I've had long chats with men I don't know over coffee or dessert, but because I knew these weren't "date dates," I felt free to say and do whatever I wanted without worrying that the guy across from me would think I was boring or crazy (mostly the latter). In other words, those non-dates were F-U-N! Not to mention I didn't shave my legs beforehand or put on mascara before I left the house. Woo-hoo!

And I've had a gentleman caller or two for dinner. By "gentleman caller," I mean a guy who calls me during dinner to pitch me a cell phone plan or health insurance. Each will start the same pick-up line, "Are you happy with your current plan?" and I'll respond in my best Lauren Bacall voice, "That depends. What are you wearing?" Hey, they're interrupting my dinner so the least they owe me is a little bit of amusement.

I used to be good at the rituals of dating. I still have a collection of twenty cocktail napkins on which I carried on a mildly hot night of flirting with a stranger in a bar years ago. Therein lies the problem, however: the last time I was in the "dating pool," we communicated via cocktail napkins instead of texts and selfies. I don't text on principal. The principal being that I can't read my cell phone without my reading glasses and by the time I find them, I've forgotten what I was going to say.

Before you start feeling sorry for me, let me give you a few important details. First, for five of the ten years I haven't dated, I was married. I don't know about you, but I'm the kind of person who believes it's unfair for married folks to hog all the good dates from the single people. I'm just *that* thoughtful.

Now that I'm single again, I'm over 50. You may be happy to know that there are men who WILL ask a woman over 50 out. I've turned a number down. The most recent guy to ask me out received the same

response I give financial planners who want to talk to me about investing—
a stuttered, "Why? What do you want?" I wasn't trying to be mean or coy, I
just blurted out the first thing that came to mind. That's another fact you
should know. I tend to say whatever I'm thinking these days.

Unfortunately, many of the men who want to date 50-somethings are
in their 80s, not that there is anything wrong with that. I just had a meeting
at a local restaurant with a woman who runs a charity. While we were
talking, an octogenarian in what appeared to be a plaid jumpsuit from the
1970s kept winking at me. He may have been recovering from a recent eye-
dilation or he may have been giving me the "come-hither" look. I no longer
know.

The other group of men who seem interested in women my age are in
their 20s. I don't date men that young because they expect me to teach them
something. It's bad enough I have to correct their grammar—I shouldn't be
expected to be Mrs. Krabappel (rest in peace, Marcia Wallace) in the
boudoir. I'm just not a cougar. I prefer the term "puma." It seems faster and
somehow thinner.}

As for men my own age, I've discovered something odd. They all
seem to want a long-term relationship. They're like 20-something women,
except they're slightly less likely to have ear buds permanently embedded
in their ear canals. I'm not looking for a long-term relationship because I've
already done that: I was married for 25 years. Well, not all to the same man.
But it still counts in my book.

If you're single and looking for Mr. or Ms. Right, have at it. Rest
assured that I'm practicing "catch and release" with any guy who expresses
an interest in me, so there are more for you. You can thank me by buying
me some dark chocolate. I'll never swear off dating them.

## A Movie-ing Thanksgiving

Families do a lot of things during the Thanksgiving holiday that they might not otherwise – they give thanks instead of posting Yelp reviews of the meal; they spend hours in line to buy a combination 65" screen TV/cellphone/robot vacuum cleaner; they pretend that marshmallows aren't a weird dinner topping…

They also frequently leave the leftovers behind and head for a local movie theater to take in a flick after the big meal. In fact, nearly one-third of Thanksgiving survivors report going to see a movie over the holiday weekend, which is slightly more than the number who spend their time rummaging through closets looking for a pair of sweat pants a size bigger.

To me, going out to the movies has always been one of the best parts about Thanksgiving, whether I was spending it with my family of origin or any of my three sets of former in-laws. Movies provide a way to be with family without having to talk to them. Now that's a win-win in my book. I am not the kind of person who can easily hold her tongue when conversation turns to politics, religion, climate change, fashion, health, animal welfare, gardening, education, dance trends, reality TV, dog-training, shaving, what Kim Kardashian does or doesn't do… anything, really. So the opportunity to sit in a dark theater after debating global warming with my some of my relatives who prefer living in denial is always welcome. I sit there in that comfy reclining seat, my feet only partially glued to the floor, and listen to my blood pressure return to "only moderately high considering how much salt you just ate." Now that's paradise.

With so much movie-viewing this time of year, you'd think there would be a lot of movies with a Thanksgiving theme. I could only come up with a few on my own, so I did some research (aka, Googled "movies about Thanksgiving"). It's a tough job, but I'm more than happy to do it.

The list that popped up included many films that left me shaking my head about the Turkey Day tie-in. Spiderman? Rocky? Alien Abduction: Incident in Lake County? Ah, yes, these bring back memories of families gathered around a Thanksgivings table expressing their gratitude that they aren't overworked super heroes, down-on-their-luck boxers, or riding in a UFO as they leave their holiday meal way, way behind on Earth. Paul Blart: Mall Cop was also on the list, but that makes sense because the main action is set around a Black Friday heist gone wrong. Then there's a little indie horror flick called ThanksKilling, in which a group of students are hunted by a demonic turkey during Thanksgiving break. Well, doesn't that seem festive? I guess that will teach those students not to serve Tofurkey.

Probably the most classic Thanksgiving movie in my mind is Planes, Trains and Automobiles with Steve Martin and John Candy. If you haven't seen it, the story focuses on two men trying to get home for Thanksgiving and the obstacles that prevent them from doing so. I find this film easier to watch in years I'm not going anywhere, however. Movies about how hard it is to reach your destination just aren't as funny when you're stuck in an airplane that has been circling the airport for an hour and the flight attendant refuses to let you use the "lavatory" despite your veiled threats, so you're binge-eating tiny pretzels and swearing that next time you need to fly, you'll just grow your own wings.

The absolute best kind of Thanksgiving movies to watch with your family are those that make you appreciate them and their unique brand of craziness because by comparison to the characters on the big screen they're not so bad. If you're like me and have ever eaten turkey in a trailer while a house-peacock watched, done the Heimlich maneuver on a brother-in-law moments after he hit on you in the garage, or found a missing turkey carcass in a stepbrother's bathtub, you know how hard script writers have to work to create truly oddball characters for their holiday movies.

So I've taken it upon myself to come up with an idea for a new Thanksgiving movie I'm calling Drop and Give Me 20 Things You're Thankful About. It goes something like this: Slightly kooky hippie mom JoAnn, her 13-year-old twin mean girls and their cat, Snarly, decide to spend Thanksgiving with her parents, both former ex-Marines. Because it's been five years since she's been home, JoAnn doesn't realize that her parents have converted their suburban home into a boot camp, and they are eagerly anticipating spending Thanksgiving putting their daughter and grandchildren, as well as three Goth twenty-somethings and a stoner, through their paces as they film everything for a reality show called "Get Your Butt Out of Bed, It's 4 a.m.!"

Now wouldn't that make you feel better about the people sitting around your table this holiday season?

**Ten Movies Harry Potter Could Star in As an Adult**

Do you think Harry had it tough as a kid? Here are the movie titles we might have seen had the series continued:

1.  Harry Potter and the Haunt of the Student Loan Officer

2.  Harry Potter and the Order of Jalapeno Poppers

3.  Harry Potter and the Acid Reflux of Fire

4.  Harry Potter and the Lawn that Needed Mowing Every Week

5.  Harry Potter and the Side Effects from Lipitor

6.  Harry Potter and the Daughter Who Loved Zombies but Was Embarrassed by Being Seen with Her Father

7.  Harry Potter and the Hallows of a Midlife Crisis

8.  Harry Potter and Sting of Male Pattern Baldness

9.  Harry Potter and Horror of Going on Dancing with the Stars

10. Harry Potter and the Chamber of Memory Loss

**This Year's Swimsuit Season Called Off**

Finally the government has done something right. Due to a sharp decline in the number of people with "bathing suit bodies," the FCC (Fashion Crime Commission) has called off this year's swimsuit season. According to a size 14 spokesperson who wished to remain anonymous, *"There's a distinct chance that the size 0-2 woman, for whom the average swimsuit is typically designed, may be facing extinction. And although we can't pinpoint a single factor, it does appear that 40 oz. triple caramel lattes and bagels the size of Volkswagen Beetles may be partially to blame. It is our hope that by allowing Americans to sit out this swimsuit season and giving them an extra year to get in shape, we can turn those numbers around before the end of the decade. "*

I am personally thrilled with the news! Not just from a personal perspective either. Just think of all the energy we can save this summer by not sucking in our stomachs for hours and spending days trying to dig too small bikini bottoms out from locations they shouldn't be in the first place. Not to mention how much we can reduce foreign oil imports by foregoing slathering ourselves with sunscreen and not having to apply Vaseline to our inner thighs to keep them from singing like crickets as we walk along the beach hoping no one we know spots us.

Now perhaps you are between the ages of 17-21 and actually look good in a two-piece made from dental floss and dryer lint. And perhaps you're thinking, *"Hey, how am I supposed to show off these toned abs that I've spent 14 hours a day doing crunches for?"* I feel for you. Really, I do (somewhere down deep. My pancreas, maybe). But let me offer you this condolence – by banning swimsuits from beaches, lakes, boardwalks, country clubs, zoos, baseball games, grocery stores, parking lots, lawyers' offices, PTA meetings, weddings, etc., you won't be traumatized by getting a glimpse of your future when you take a gander at the rest of us who really, really should (and want to) stay covered up all year 'round. Muffin tops, spare tires, thunder thighs, butterfly tattoos that have metamorphosed into scary monster faces due to the effects of gravity… these are just a few of the sights no one should have to see. Not even in the mirror at home. Which is why I usually shower in a blindfold. It does wonders for my self-esteem.

And if this is the way I – a size 8 most days and without any extra skin hanging down around my knees after stomach stapling or a scar running down my midsection from open heart surgery – feel, I can't imagine the horror people who are heavier and older than I face when the days start to get longer and hotter and lakeside vacations and water skiing and days lounging by the pool loom ahead. It's no wonder all we have Post Traumatic Swimsuit Disorder.

And let's face it, no matter how much the swimsuit industry would like us to believe that this year's *miracle* fabric can "makes your tummy disappear and takes 15 pounds off your derriere," there are no such miracles. Fat that disappears from somewhere is going to spill out somewhere else, according to the laws of physics (the only laws I always obey). If your butt and stomach are flat, but there's 15 pounds of skin and fat flapping around under your arm pits, this is not attractive. Perhaps if designers would come up with a swimsuit made out of tiny little mirrors that reflect light like a disco ball and keep anyone from looking directly at us, that might work. Or a suit that has a digital chip imbedded in it that flashes subliminal messages like "Tell the wearer of this suit she's hot and sexy." That'd be good too.

But until technology catches up with us (which should be easy to do since we're not moving as quickly as we used to), let's just sit this one out. Don't worry about the fact that your 6-pack abs are now looking more like a keg. Stop being paranoid that something is following you and you think it's your back fat. Just put on your baggy t-shirt and Capri pants and save yourself the stress. After all you've got a whole year to get in shape. Lattes and bagels all around!

**Out of this World Weddings**

Sometime next year a woman I know is planning to get married in space. She's already put the down payment on a rocket plane (a modified Lear Jet) that will reach an altitude of 300,000 feet where she and her groom will say "I do" free from the pull of the earth's gravity. Needless to say, I won't be in the wedding party. Not only do I get queasy during the take-off of a regular flight, I also refuse to wear the bridesmaid's spacesuit with the puffy sleeves and giant bow on the back side.

Although it definitely is NOT the wedding of my dreams, I can see how getting hitched 62 miles above the earth might have its advantages. Every woman I know wants to lose weight in time for the big day, so what could be better than actually being weightless when you exchange your vows? For brides who want to cut down on their guest list, an extraterrestrial wedding is just the ticket. Not to mention how getting married off the planet relieves the pressure of finding a really special place to honeymoon.

A space wedding starts at around $500,000 for the basic package – no flowers, no candles, no harpist, no birdseed tossed at the bride following the ceremony. Additionally, some extra precautions have to be taken: the bride will have to make adjustments to her gown to make sure it doesn't float above her head mid-vow, for example. If ever there was at time for Velcro, this is it. Her groom may also have to have Dramamine patches sewn into his tux.

Fortunately, most brides-to-be are more down-to-earth when it comes to their own dream wedding. Even a Renaissance wedding on horseback or underwater nuptials in Hawaii don't require the happy couple to endure G-force training or practice emergency ejections at NASA.

Despite all the planning and striving for the perfect fairy tale nuptials, of the nearly fifty weddings I've attended in my life, the two I remember best were among the simplest. The first was a small ceremony attended by just a handful of family and friends. The only members of the official wedding party were the ring bearer and flower girl; he was adorable in his tux and she in her pink taffeta with tiny freshwater pearls at the collar. The guests were reduced to smiles and giggles as the pair paraded down the aisle following a trail of kibble. Bailey, the ring bearer was a four year-old Black Lab, and Maggie, the flower girl, a ten year-old Australian Shepherd.

Not only were the canine members of the family part of the celebration, they also joined in the reception afterward. Begging for "Pigs in a Blanket" and hot wings was followed by a spin on the dance floor as the bride and groom had their first dance as husband and wife. The bride's gown ended up covered with dog hair from the knees down, but that Labrador could really cut a rug.

My other favorite wedding was a Sufi ceremony at Island Park in Springfield. I wasn't sure what to expect, not really knowing what "Sufi" was. I inquired and was told that it is a spiritual practice that celebrates truth and honors every form of worship in which the unity of religious ideals is respected. And that I should wear whatever I would wear to the Oregon Country Fair.

Needless to say, this wedding was one of the most colorful I've been to, with floral sundresses and tie-dyed jackets and socks. The footwear was also the most comfortable I've ever worn to a wedding. What was most memorable was that all of the guests were part of the wedding ceremony – we joined hands in a large circle and chanted and danced around the bride and groom as they committed their lives to one another. As someone who never passes up an opportunity to sing or dance (just ask anyone who has ever caught me mid-Broadway production in a public bathroom), I thoroughly enjoyed myself.

Perhaps the reason I have such fond memories of this wedding, however, is that right next to us in the park that day the area Ferret Club was hosting some kind of Ferret Olympics. Every time our circle of dancers moved and I ended up facing the sixty or so ferrets running over hurdles and swinging from mini-trapezes, I couldn't help but laugh and smile. Sunshine, music and dancing, and four-footed creatures behaving in entirely unceremonious ways. And no one had to strap themselves in for re-entry afterward. Ah, now that's the perfect wedding.

## Judge Fifi, Canine Court*

*The bailiff, a bull mastiff calls the court to order and sniffs both the plaintiff, Maddy Lou, and the defendant, Justin, for honesty and liver snaps. Judge Fifi, dressed in a black collar, leaps up onto her stool, bites at a few fleas and addresses the courtroom.*

Judy Fifi: Before we begin, let me just admonish both parties that I don't tolerate whining in my courtroom. Okay, I'll listen to the complainant first. Maddy Lou, you are seeking punitive damages in the amount of $15 and mental distress damages in the amount of $2.3 million or a lifetime supply of dog cookies from the defendant, Justin. Is that correct?

*Maddy Lou and Justin, both dachshunds, stand behind their respective dachshund-sized podiums, and refer to their notes. Maddy Lou holds a stuffed bear in her mouth and says something, but the actual words are muffled.*

Judge Fifi: What?

*Maddy Lou drops the bear on the floor.*

Maddy Lou: Sorry, your honor. I've brought this stuffed bear, named "Bear," as Exhibit A.

*Judge Fifi points to a suspicious looking spot on the floor of the courtroom.*

Judge Fifi: I thought that was Exhibit A.

Maddy Lou: (embarrassed) No, I just got really nervous, your honor.

Judge Fifi: Bailiff bring me the bear. And watch your step.

*The bailiff takes the bear to Judge Fifi, who examines it. Its face has been ripped off and replaced by a large denim patch. There are teeth marks all over its body.*

Judge Fifi:  I'd say this bear has seen better days. What's your complaint?

Maddy Lou:  This bear has been in my family for four years, although it seems like twenty-eight, way longer than the defendant.

*To reiterate her point, Maddy Lou nips at Justin. Moving quickly, he avoids her bite.*

Justin:  She's out of control, your honor.

Judge Fifi:  Do that again and I'll have to issue a gag order, I mean, a muzzle order.  You may continue.

Maddy Lou:  This is Bear. I've had him all my life. I play fetch with him. I sleep on him. I snuggle with him after meals. Bear is very, very important to me.

Judge Fifi:  Point taken. And you claim that the defendant...?

Maddy Lou:  Ever since he joined the family, and believe me, I was not consulted about the matter, he's just taken over. He hounds, he whines, he steals my stuff. He's got at least fifty toys – mailmen, cats, an octopus...

Judge Fifi:  An octopus?  Does it have eight squeakers?

*Judge Fifi drools a little.*

Maddy Lou:  It did until he ripped them out!  He's got more than enough toys of his own and I've only got Bear. I love Bear.

Judge Fifi:  Are you claiming that the defendant is responsible for the extensive damage to this bear?  The holes, the ripped limbs, the missing face?

Maddy Lou:  Well, no, I did that. Sometimes you hurt the ones you love.

Judge Fifi:  Yeah, I know how that is. I once had this stuffed lawyer... Well, anyway, what exactly are you seeking damages for?

Maddy Lou:  For his constant thievery.

Justin: I object. I don't steal. I borrow.

Judge Fifi:  Quiet. You'll get your doggone turn.

Maddy Lou.  It's awful. I'll be playing a nice game of fetch with one of my humans, and before I know what's happened, Justin's got Bear in his mouth and is frolicking down the hallway like he owns the world. At least twice, he's taken Bear outside where he got rained on!

Judge Fifi:  Have you told him to leave your bear alone?

Maddy Lou:  Of course, your honor, but he doesn't listen. He cocks his head to one side and pretends to listen, but it goes in one floppy ear and...

*Justin cocks his head to one side, pretending to listen.*

Judge Fifi:  I see. Okay, Justin, let me hear your side of the story. Why do you insist on taking plaintiff's bear away from her.

Justin:  What? Me? What was the question?

Judge Fifi:  Why do you keep taking the bear from your sister?

Justin: It's for her own good, your honor.

Judge Fifi: Care to explain?

Justin: She's obsessed with this bear. I occasionally take the silly thing away from her to get her to see there are other options out there. Stuffed rabbits, squirrels, hedgehogs... heck, I've even offered her a stuffed cow that moos when you bite it. But nooo... she's fixated on the one mangy bear.

Maddy Lou: My bear does not have mange, your honor.

*Judge Fifi holds up Bear to examine it more closely. Maddy Lou leaps across the courtroom (t takes her seven or eight leaps, as her legs are very short), grab the bear and runs out of the courtroom.*

Judge Fifi: Well, it seems we no longer have a plaintiff or Exhibit A. Not to mention that it's way past my naptime. Case dismissed.

Justin: Can I meet you in your chambers, Judge?

Judge Fifi: For what purpose?

Justin: I'd just like to see your collection of stuffed animals...

*This column is written in memory of my sweet dog Maddy Lou who went over the rainbow bridge three years ago this month.

## Fun with Medical Technology

I recently had to have a CAT scan because my doctor thought I might have kidney stones. Now those are two words that don't belong together – kidney and stones. One is supposed to be inside your body and the other lying around in the yard somewhere. What's next, liver trees? Duodenal birdbaths?

I knew from watching Gray's Anatomy and Scrubs tat CAT scans don't involve cats (a shame if you ask me; what medical procedure wouldn't be improved if you could hold a purring feline on your lap? Or have one dig his claws into the doctor?) CAT scans do involve lying completely still, not breathing, and being very quiet. I'm not good at any of these—which is why I flunked obedience training.

I scored the lowest marks on the not breathing part, but it wasn't my fault. Eric, the sullen technician who apparently couldn't be bothered to brush his hair, plopped me down on the cold hard table and explained the procedure. "…slide you in… blah blah blah… hold completely still… blah blah blah… I hate this job and as soon as I win the lottery I'm outta here…" Excellent. Just what you want for a major diagnostic procedure – a guy having both a bad life and a bad hair day.

As he walked back toward the booth with three-foot thick steel walls protecting him from the kryptonite or whatever he was about to shoot through my body, he mumbled, "Oh, and you'll have to hold your breath as long as possible when I say 'Now!'" He said the last word so loudly I practically jumped up off the table. But at least the shock warmed me up a little. Because, let's face it, that backless paper gown wasn't really doing much to keep my body heat in.

I hate holding my breath because I have lousy lung capacity – I can't even blow bubbles without getting winded. I don't really understand it because I've never smoked and I get plenty of exercise. I think the problem is my lungs are the size of thimbles. I don't have proof because they'd have to do an x-ray and I can't hold my breath long enough for them to get a clean picture.

You'd think that if you're going to have to hold your breath for a medical procedure you'd get a little advance warning: "Okay in five, four, three, two, one…" But no, I had just finished exhaling (and readjusting the gown so that the naked part of me was on the table and not on display to anyone who happened to walk in to tell Eric his lottery ticket was a dud) when I heard the word "Now!" come from behind the wall.

I tried not to breathe. Really I did. I tried to visualize myself underwater in Australia looking at the Great Barrier Reef or being out in space floating around the rings of Saturn. Nothing worked. I think I held my breath approximately .00027 seconds before I started gasping for air like a goldfish who has been unceremoniously dumped from her bowl onto the cold floor.

After I got a few good gulps of air in me, I started to suggest that Eric let me know in advance when he was ready so that I could fill my lungs with air first. Unfortunately, before I could finish the though, he yelled "Now!" again. Great. I breathed immediately. I really had no choice. It was either breathe or die, and I figured I'd rather have a kidney stone than a headstone.

Fortunately, I got one more chance and it would have turned out okay except for the hiccoughs. Again, it wasn't my fault. I get them whenever I get nervous. And this whole procedure was making me very nervous. I was afraid that not only would they not be able to interpret the CAT Scan ("I can't tell, is that a kidney or a map of the Congo?"), my failure at the test would go on my permanent record, along with the time I cheated in algebra and those three days in junior high I said I had the flu, but I was really home learning how to apply make-up.

The good news is, they're pretty sure I don't have a kidney stone. The bad news is, they want to do the CAT scan one more time just to confirm things. I get breathless just thinking about it.

## Just the Flax

On the advice of this guy I sat next to at the Department of Motor Vehicles, I've started adding flax and chia seeds to everything I eat. They're both tasty when sprinkled on cereal and baked into cookies (mmmh, cookies), but I have to say it's hard to get the seeds to adhere to carrot sticks unless I slather them with cream cheese or peanut butter first. I'm sure that's heart-healthy, right? Besides, as far as I know, no one's made flax butter yet.

One thing no one warned me about was that these tiny seeds may be good for my body, but they're hell on my gums. And I'm not just talking about a few seeds stuck between random teeth (not a good look, but I could live with that). The problem is, like many middle-aged people, I have flabby gums. The tight, firm gums that used to turn heads in college have been replaced by droopy, saggy things that shock my dentist when I show up at her office every three years. I'd go more often, but my self-esteem suffers every time she uses a yardstick to measure just how deep the "gum pockets" are. It doesn't help that she calls out the numbers in the metric system. "4,117 millimeters, whoa!"

Needless to say, with a virtual Carlsbad Cavern cave system under my teeth, it's easy for tiny flax or tinier chia seeds to get stuck in there. That is not to say I haven't also lost a piece of coconut, a chocolate chip, or a hiker, but those are big enough to floss out.

What I really need -- and I know I'm not alone here -- is some kind of exercise program to tighten up my sedentary gums. If you can work out your triceps and gluts, why not your gum line? I tried to develop such a program on my own, but apparently a 30-minute routine of smiling like a chimpanzee then puckering like a llama about to spit, is useless. Well, not entirely. I did make a few new friends on the bus.

If you're a dental professional looking for a way to boost business, please don't ignore the flabby-gummed. We need some kind of workout device and the Gumerciser may just be your ticket to a stint on the Home Shopping Network.

## Crazy Dog Lady

Occasionally I ask myself, "Have I officially become a 'Crazy Dog Lady'?"

The question really bothers me, but not for the reasons you might think. You see, I want to be the crazy dog lady. In fact, I thought I had secured the title in the early 90s when I retrofitted a baby stroller for Copper, my 15-year-old dachshund who could no longer trot at the speed he preferred. People pointed and laughed as I jogged past them, pushing a gray-muzzled wiener dog in front of me. When I hired someone to build a ramp so that both Copper and his brother Slate could get onto the sofa without hurting their backs, I'm fairly sure I heard the contractor snort with derision. I'm not 100% certain because I was on the phone with the American Dogs with Disabilities Association checking the maximum allowable slope.

Today, however, you can buy both dog strollers and ramps in catalogs and online. Surveys show that two-thirds of us buy gifts for our pets for their birthdays and other holidays, while over half of us talk to our animals on the phone when we're away from home. There are also thousands of people who plan to leave the bulk of their estate (which, in my case, consists of a good comfortable chair and forty-seven pairs of sunglasses) to their companion animals. Where once I was off the deep end, dog-wise, the rest of the world has caught up with me and now I seem to be almost normal.

"Normal" is not a group I aspire to belong to, so I'd like to petition the court to consider my other unusual dog-related behavior:

- I picked out the vinyl tiles for my kitchen by sliding across them in my stocking feet at the store in order to make sure the dogs wouldn't slip while begging for their Hoggin' Dogs ice cream.
- I gave up ironing twelve years ago because one of my dogs hated the sound the ironing board made when I opened and closed it. I see no reason to take it up again this late in life.
- I have been known to interrupt a human conversation with the phrase, "Look, a squirrel!"
- I feel the need to put the word "human" before "conversation" to distinguish it from the canine conversations I more frequently have.

If that's not enough to earn me the title, I'm willing to do whatever it takes. I'll have to work fast, though. I just heard a report on the radio that said that 70% of women would marry their dogs if they could. Now THAT's crazy!

## Too Cool for School

It's the first day of eighth grade and I'm walking to Bitburg American High School, kicking up rocks with brown-loafered feet, hoping I don't dirty my white knee socks. I'm feeling stylish in a new magenta dress with tiny golden pigs on it and a golden bow tie at the neck. My hair is very short, with my bangs swept to one side to keep them off my military-issue squared-off black plastic glasses. More than anything, I'm hoping the kids at this new school like me and aren't intimidated by superior fashion sense. Tiny golden pigs and a bow tie? I should have been walking a runway, not a sidewalk to school.

I remember that day and those feelings as if they happened yesterday, which is odd because I have no memory of what actually happened yesterday. I do, however, know there was chocolate involved. There always is.

Flash forward to today. Kids are heading to back to school and trying to decide what Glee cast member to dress and act like this year. But we grown-ups forget how important clothing really is in the daily fashion show of middle school and high school. Every day is a test of where you fit in, and if you slip up just once and wear, say, an orange mohair dickey under a t-shirt because your stepmother insists it will help keep you from catching cold, you could be laughed off the cheerleading squad and end up smoking under the bleachers instead. Don't ask me how I know.

Fashions may change, but the pressure to look good doesn't. Fortunately, teens these days have more options for expressing themselves than we did back at Bitburg Junior High. A quick look at my yearbook proves how limited our choices were. I paged through all 130 pages and saw no tattoos, no Goth ensembles, and no funny t-shirts with slogans such as "Zombies rule," "Sarcasm: Just another service I offer," or "You looked hotter on Facebook." In fact there were no t-shirts in my school at all! Not even on the boys, who all wore button-down shirts or turtlenecks... even while playing basketball. Yes, our team did lose most of its games, but the players looked very Beatnik in their photos and really, that's what mattered.

Jumpers were the clearly the trendy must-have in 1970 (please don't tell my mom I'm this old; it will kill her). Back then a jumper was a one-piece sleeveless dress that was worn over a puffy-sleeved blouse (that's right, we wore puffy pirate shirts long before Jerry Seinfeld made them unpopular). Our jumpers were ill-fitting and oversized, as was everything, even our underwear.

I could find only one photo of a girl wearing pants. I believe she was either in a play or an exchange student from Russia.

Plaid was VERY popular that year. From plaid shirts to plaid vests to plaid ponchos to plaid prom dresses. That's right, prom dresses! This may explain why even today every time I dance, I itch. Skirts were short, shoes were flat and teachers wore suits and ties or dresses and pearls. Except for Ms. Bartz who wore a dress and tie. She was our very own Annie Hall and we loved her for it.

The boys hairstyles were Beatles-inspired, while most of the girls had long straight hair held back with ribbons and barrettes. My short do was the trend-setting result of my dad testing out a new electric razor the week before school started. I may have looked out of place, but at least I fared better than our dog, who was shunned by the other canines in the dog park. I jest; there was no such thing as a dog park. Nor did he have the option of donning a cute doggy sweater until his locks grew out. Even his fashion choices were limited.

Perhaps the biggest fashion difference between then and now is in what we girls were required to wear to gym class. We weren't allowed to wear sweats and a hoodie or shorts and a t-shirt. We had to… well, I'm just going to go ahead and spit it out… we had to wear a white snap-front blouse and… bloomers. That's right, bloomers – navy blue shorts that came to our knees and puffed out at the hips and thighs. Our lower halves looked like unfilled bean bag chairs. If you filled our bloomers with sand and stood us side by side, we could have kept our small German village from flooding whenever the river rose.

The lesson I've learned from this quick trip down fashion memory lane is that no matter how dorky and itchy we looked and felt, we all made it out alive. So if you have a 'tween or teen who is self-conscious about what to wear to school this fall, Google the word "cotton bloomers" and show the photo to your kid. Tell her my story. She'll head off to school in her Twilight-inspired ensemble or Katy Perry outfit feeling much better about herself... as long as you don't cut her hair yourself.

**Your Surreal Age**

Aging experts now say that chronological age doesn't really matter in the overall scheme of things. What's really important is biological age – a combination of your current health, genetic and environmental health risks, and how many times you flunked biology in high school. Okay, the last one not so much, but it should count for something. Your biological age is also known as your "real age." Just don't try telling that to the people at the Social Security Administration. Believe me on this.

Just out of curiosity – and because none of my Facebook friends were doing anything interesting enough to distract me from work – I took an online test to prove how young I really am. The test didn't require me to feed a virtual pony or crush any candy, so I figured what could it hurt?

There were 200 questions and after each section, the computer would recalculate my age so that I could see just how certain behaviors and genetic factors affected me. After I answered that I've never smoked, always wear a seat belt even on my bicycle, exercise regularly (if my "regular" you mean "I can remember the last time"), and still remember my maiden name as well as all my married names, the computer calculated my biological age was nearly eleven years younger than my chronological age. Good, but not good enough. Especially since Wii had told me earlier than morning I was only 33. I trust him because he knows how much I weigh.

The test then asked me about my cholesterol level, how often I ride in a car without airbags, and whether I'd ever been the target of a lawsuit. Apparently, frequent exposure to the legal system can age you faster than chain-smoking cigars while speeding down the highway in an old Pinto with a bag of giant vegan marshmallows in your lap to cushion the blow in an accident.

I was doing great until I flunked one part of the test. Suddenly I aged six and a half years. Talk about a strict grading system. The section I blew dealt with how much time I have spent sitting in airports in the past five years. I always knew that every 30 minutes spent in an airport listening to people yell into their cell phones about how their flight had been delayed adds 6 months to your age – now I have proof. This is one of the reasons I gave up flying this year. That and the fact that I can no longer pretend to believe that my seat cushion can serve as a flotation device when it doesn't even serve as a seat cushioning device.

Finally, I finished all the questions and when my overall biological age popped on the screen, I was only four years younger than I really am. That stressed me out and caused my heart to pound and my blood pressure to shoot up to at least 110/75. That may not sound bad to you, but that's dangerous for me.

When I calmed down (after coloring in my Winnie the Pooh coloring book for an hour and singing The Wheels on the Bus seven times), I realized the test was clearly defective. Somehow a whole section dealing with mental age had been omitted. Everyone knows that age is a state of mind, yet where were the questions about that? In my youthful opinion, the missing section should have included the following:

When was the last time someone told you to grow up and act your age?

How many wind-up toys do you have on your desk?

How often do you skip to meetings?

How long has it been since you last took recess?

When was the last time you stuck your tongue out when you were mad?

Which one of your friends has cooties?

These are questions I know I would ace. So I've done a little recalculating of my own and do you know what? My biological age is seven and a half. And if you argue with me, I'm going to tell your mom on you.

*Don't Laugh! You'll Wake the Dog*

## A Fun Holiday Brain Game

Scientists have decided that men and women really are different. I know. I'm as shocked as you are... said no one ever.

The news you may not know is that brain researchers say there is a typical female brain (which is pink and smells like chocolate) and a typical male brain (which usually has a sports team logo branded on the side). Interestingly enough, apparently about 10-15% of men are born with a female brain, while 10% of women have one that wants to take apart a carburetor for the fun of it.

Studies have shown that the frontal lobe and limbic cortex are much bigger in women, while the parietal cortex and amygdala are bigger in men. If the word "bigger" made you grunt and pump your fist in the air, you know what kind of brain you have. Men also have more gray matter, while women have more white (or buttermilk, ecru, winter white, or ivory, depending upon the time of day and angle of the sun).

I don't know about you, but I don't have easy access to an MRI and can't readily scan the brains of my loved ones. There must be an easier way to determine what kind of gray matter everyone in your social circle has and I'm here to offer you the **Jasheway Holiday Brain Test and Gingerbread Cookie Recipe** (patent pending). I may not be a scientist, but I've watched enough Big Bang Theory reruns to feel qualified to provide you with the tools to finally, once and for all, settle why the people who drop in for Hanukkah, Winter Solstice, Christmas, Kwanzaa, and Jimmy Buffet's Birthday (December 26) are the way there are.

To use the **Jasheway Holiday Brain Test and Gingerbread Cookie Recipe** (trademarked, registered, and AKC papers filed), simply corner a friend or family member and subject them to the following simple process:

1. Point to a calendar and show how little time there is between today and whatever winter holiday(s) your family celebrates. Note your loved one's response. Does he/she: (a) hyperventilate and mumble,

"I'll never get it all done"; (b) roll eyes and shrug; or (c) grab another fistful of chips and attempt to get a better view of the giant TV screen by leaning in one direction?

2.  Suggest to your loved one that it's time to decorate the house. Does he /she: (a) immediately begin a craft project that involves velvet ribbon, pinecones, and yogurt containers; (b) continue to press buttons on a gaming device until all the angry birds are only slightly frustrated; or (c) offer to clear the moss off the roof using the riding lawn mower after the game is over?

3.  Insist that your loved one join you for a trip to the mall to knock out the rest of the holiday shopping. Does he/she: (a) smile in a way that frightens you and the dog; (b) say "I'll go, but don't stand within 100 feet of me;" or (c) duct tape him/herself to the garage door?

4.  Slice a piece of fruitcake and ask your loved one to describe what he/she sees when staring at the gelatinous fruit-like thingies. Is the response: (a) "Mrs. Claus, who is clearly doing all the work and getting none of the credit"; (b) "An extended curfew for Hanukkah"; or (c) "That hot girl from Fringe."

5.  Hand your guinea pig, I mean, test subject, this recipe:

**Gingerbread Cookie Recipe**
3 cups of flour, half all purpose and half graham
1/2 teaspoon salt, preferably sea salt from the nearest sea so that you
don't feel guilty about how much fuel was consumed to get it to you
3/4 teaspoon baking soda
2 teaspoons freshly ground ginger
1 teaspoon cinnamon, ground, not stick even though it is fun to pretend
to be a walrus with the sticks
1/4 teaspoon ground cloves (no, you may not substitute garlic)
1/2 cup Caucasian sugar, or if you prefer, Agave nectar
1 large egg, preferably free-range, hormone-free, and you know the
chicken's name…

Once the recipe has been read, does your loved one: (a) start dialing
neighbors to see whose chickens have eggs available; (b) say, "Is there
any leftover pizza?" or (c) fall to the floor because his or her brains have
actually exploded?

Score the test by assigning 1 point for each *a* answer, 2 for each *b*, and
3 for each *c*. A score of 1-5 means you're dealing with a female brain all the
way. Chances are this brain, while taking this test, also wrote six to-do lists,
folded the laundry, and negotiated peace with two or more warring nations.
A score of 6-12 means you're dealing with a classic teenage brain. "Real"
scientists may not acknowledge this as a separate type of brain, but come
on, you know it is. A score of 13 and higher is a classic male brain, which
still after taking this test, seeing the holiday decorations go up, smelling the
hot apple cider on the stove, and greeting distant relatives at the door has no
idea the holidays are right around the corner.

There you have it, a great way to pass the time and learn about the
people in your life. In the end, however, no matter whose brain you have,
please enjoy your holidays without losing your mind.

**Party On**

I have never been much of a party animal. Really, I'm more like a party eggplant – I'm shiny and happy (and often purple) in the sunlight, but when the sun goes down, I prefer to hide in the shadows. My idea of a rollicking good time usually includes my getting home by 9:30 p.m. to read the next chapter of whatever book I'm engrossed in with three sleeping dachshunds on my lap. Woo-hoo!

Part of my party aversion is that most grown-up soirees are held at night, which in my opinion, is a darned shame. Why should 5-year-olds get to have cake, play with piñatas, and get buzzed on juice boxes in the middle of the afternoon while we grown-ups have to wait until the sun goes down to have fun? How do you even find a piñata in the dark?

My early birdiness was clear by the time I was a teenager. Other kids my age begged their parents to give them later curfews so they could go party with their friends all night long. I, having gotten up at daybreak, insisted on an early curfew so I could get my shut-eye and be ready for a long school day ahead. I think I was born with Amish biorhythms. Up and down with the sun. That may also explain the little beard that's been trying to grow in…

Adult activities also seem to involve alcohol much of the time and I'm not much of a drinker. Well, I do all right with water, but anything stronger just makes me sleepy. I went to high school in a small, dry Texas town. By dry, I don't mean filled with tumbleweeds (although on certain days, that was the case); instead, it was filled with pious people who looked back fondly on the days of Prohibition. Remember the movie Footloose? No drinking, no dancing, no fun-having of any kind? That film could easily have been filmed in my hometown of Abilene, Texas in the 70s, except I don't remember anyone as good-looking as Kevin Bacon …and I've scoured my yearbooks several times just in case I missed him.

The first time I had a sip of alcohol, it was Crème de Menthe from a friend's parents' private liquor collection. It tasted like someone has swished toothpaste around in mouthwash – not a bad taste for teeth-cleaning, but not anything I wanted to make a habit of.

After high school, I went to The University of Texas at Austin. It wasn't until my junior year that I discovered that it was party school. I thought they had said "arty school" and that was cool. I'd love to have painted the campus red, okay, burnt orange, but only while sober and during daylight hours. Instead, I spent my time debating and calculating stuff with my ever-present slide rule. Needless to say, I wasn't invited to a lot of parties, so it all worked out.

In fact, I only remember going to two parties in my college days. The first was held in my roommate and my 350-square-foot apartment. We had invited 15 people over, they all got drunk and one of them proceeded to de-tinsel our tiny Christmas tree, one strand at a time. Then he danced with it. The second party was thrown by my debate coach and included fellow debaters (now those are some party animals!) and my coach's friends. He had just installed a quadraphonic speaker system… go ahead, Google it, I'll wait… with speakers the size of most New York City apartments. (Funny that back then, big speakers were considered cool and now college students prefer theirs so small they could accidentally swallow them during lunch.) After listening to The Who at full volume for two hours that night, I lost part of my hearing and most of my desire to party. Really, give me a piñata and a juice box any day.

I don't begrudge others their parties that last until 2 a.m., filled with drinking and dancing and partial hearing loss. Momentous occasions in life deserve to be celebrated in the grandest fashion. But if I RSVP "No thank you" to your party that starts at 10 p.m. and runs until "Whenever the cops are called," don't think it's because I'm old and lame. I was young and lame once. On the other hand, if your shindig starts at noon and included cupcakes and running through a park giggling, I'll be your party eggplant!

## Second Time Around

I have a simple fashion philosophy: if I'm going to wear clothing from a previous decade, I don't want to spend more than I did the first time around. That's why I prefer coupon day at second-hand stores. And rooting through "free" boxes after garage sales.

Last week, a woman spotted me from the other side of the street and came rushing towards me. "Those pants!" she said breathlessly, "where'd you get those pants?" I was wearing a pair of 80s turquoise parachute pants with an Egyptian hieroglyphic pattern, which is not a look everyone can pull off. I was just about to tell her I got them at my local Goodwill store on sale for half-price when she grabbed the fabric at my knee and gushed, "I was wearing pants like these when I met my husband. Would you sell them to me?"

Can you find these pants new at the stores this season? You cannot! And where can you find an orange satin dress with black bow the size of a big-screen TV on the back (a bridesmaids gown for a Halloween wedding perhaps?), a pair of camouflage pants with fringe on the sides, and a sweatshirt with the photo and signatures of the original cast of Charlie's Angels? Not on the fashion runways, that's certain. But they're all available at thrift stores right now.

Once while volunteering at a fun run on a crisp autumn morning, I was warm and toasty in a funky purple, pink, and turquoise flannel shirt circa mid-90s. The guy running the water station approached me and said, "Excuse me, but I think you're wearing my shirt." I have to admit this was a pick-up line I'd never heard before. "I'm sorry, but what?" I asked in my natural state of confusion. "My shirt. Notice how that one button is metal and the rest are plastic? I sewed on that button myself." Not only do you get to meet interesting people when you buy used, you might even meet guys who can sew!

Shopping secondhand, I get to choose fashions from any decade and save money too. There is nothing like the sense of pride I feel when someone pays me a compliment on my cheap clothing. It's one thing having someone praise your $250 blouse (not that I know from personal experience, mind you); quite another if the blouse cost you $2.49. A woman came up to me once at an interstate rest stop and said she loved my jacket. I immediately felt both more attractive and financially astute. When's the last time that's happened to you at a rest stop?

So the next time you're in the mood for a fashion flashback, head to a thrift store. Just stay away from that orange and black bridesmaid's gown. I've got a high school reunion coming up and it's mine, mine, mine!

## Working Out is Hard to Do

Some of us went to school when P.E. classes were required. Remember P.E.? I do. In my high school Phys Ed class, all the girls had to dress in white snap-front blouses and navy bloomers. That's right, I said bloomers. If you don't know what a bloomer was, think shorts shaped like the sleeves of a pirate's shirt. Lovely, no? My P.E. uniform was even more special because back then I never went anywhere without my slide rule. If you'd seen me wearing bloomers with a slide rule attached to the waist, you'd understand why I didn't start dating until college. Even then, it was only because I found someone even more nerdy and unfashionable.

We rotated between sports in my high school P.E. class. There was softball, basketball, dodge ball, tennis... all sports in which a ball is hurled at a high rate of speed towards your head. I guess the theory was that if you survived, you had what it took to make it in the real world. I, however, tended to run screaming in what I thought was the opposite direction, but always ended up being the direct path of whatever round thing had been pitched at me. I'm lucky to have gotten out alive.

When I was a junior, we had the option of taking gymnastics. I was klutzy and not all that flexible, but at least nothing was being thrown at me, so I joined the gymnastics squad. My best event was the vault over the "horse." I had always wanted a horse and this was clearly the closest I was going to get.

After college, aerobics was the rage because the people who had invented Spandex needed a group of people who would be willing to wear it out in public. I not only took classes, I taught them for twelve years. I was that overly perky, no-pain-no-gain woman in a gold unitard and a purple headband that we all love to mock now. Three times a week, I made a gym full of mostly women sweat through their make-up and moan about how much their quads hurt. A pregnant woman's water once broke during my class and I was able to clean it up, call her doctor, and not miss a beat in the Wham song booming from my tape player.

There were a few years when I ran, despite the fact that my run is really more of a mosey. That's what happens when you spend too much time in the Deep South. I participated in marathons, but I was one of the slowest finishers in every race. Perhaps it's because I trained with wiener dogs (they kept complaining that I was holding them back.) I once finished a race behind both a man jumping rope and a woman with a walker.

My exercise "career" has also included at least a dozen pieces of home equipment. I've "invested in" a treadmill, stationary bike with air resistance (which blew so much air I looked like a dog with her head out the window), rowing machine, Bow-Flex, four different ab work devices, and "The Slide" (a piece of plastic you "skated" on in your stocking feet. I used to generate enough static electricity to power my Walkman, a personal listening device that was 4 x as big and heavy as an iPod). Apparently, I find it harder to commit to an exercise program than to a hair color."

I am older, wiser, and lazier now. Parts of my body that used to work in certain ways no longer do. Case in point: two years ago, on a whim, I went to the nearby playground and hung upside down by my knees from the monkey bars. I was unable to get down without assistance from a 7-year-old and his mom because my rotator cuff no longer rotates. Not without a can of WD-40.

These days I walk my wiener dogs now (different dogs, same short legs). I own an elliptical machine, but it bores me. I'm much happier working out with a Hippity Hop ball. You remember that from childhood, right? It's a giant rubber ball with a handle. Bouncing up and down on one in my living room while watching Dancing with the Stars has given me thighs of steel (okay, maybe quads of aluminum).

I used to believe in "No pain, no gain" and "Move it or lose it." These days, I'm happier with "If it aches, take a break." That being said, I'm still willing to give almost any new exercise trend a try – as long as I don't have to wear Spandex.

**April Showers**

You know what they say, "April showers bring… a lot of damp people with glowers." Okay, maybe that's not the cliché, but it certainly seems that rain is more annoying to more people in springtime than in fall and winter. At least it appears that way in the grocery store and the credit union as I watch folks who shake themselves dry like two-footed Golden Retrievers looking for a warm carpet to roll around on.

I, on the other hand, love living in a place with four distinct seasons – even if those seasons are rain, heavy rain, drizzle and road construction. (Maybe the cliché should be: April showers bring May road construction.") I think most people look better – and younger and thinner – wet. I know I do. Plus, who couldn't use another two or three months of free moisturizer?

One of my friends recently posted a new word on Facebook the other day: *Pluviophile*. This is a mash-up of "pluvial" (characterized by abundant rain) and "phile" (lover of). *Pluviophile* would then mean a lover of rain or someone who finds peace and joy in rainy days. What a great word to characterize many of us in the Pacific Northwest. Of course, there are those who would beg to differ, including many students at the University of Oregon who are just tolerating the gray days long enough to get a degree and head back to the land where the phrase "liquid sun" means "Pina Colada." And wiener dogs. Sometimes when it is wet out and my dogs and I are going for a walk (or to be more truthful, a drag), they stare up at me with a glower that clearly says, "Are you sure we can't afford to live in California?"

I'm writing about rain because at this very moment I'm standing at my sit-stand desk under my skylight listening to the pitter patter of drops hitting glass. It's such a beautiful sound; there should be a song about it. Oh, wait, there is. Simon and Garfunkel's, "Kathy's Song," which starts, "I hear the drizzle of the rain, like a memory it falls, soft and warm continuing, tapping on my roof and walls." This is one of the few songs I can play on my guitar. And by play, I mean "ruin." Oddly enough, many of the songs I know by heart are about rain, including Here Comes the Rain Again by the Eurythmics, Purple Rain by Prince, and It's Raining Men by... well, many women I know who regularly sing karaoke after drinking just a little too much.

As much as I love dashing through April's precipitation, I have to admit that a long period of it, say forty days and forty nights , would probably push even my buttons. Even optimists such as myself might find it hard to hold out hope for drier days after, say, 33 days of constant downpours, especially if meteorologists had just thrown up their hands and said, "Forget your umbrella, better start growing some gills." Having lots of animals to cuddle up with, however, would definitely help. By the way, were there wiener dogs on the ark? If so, did the barking ever stop?

But catastrophic rainfall aside, I'm going to stick to my pluviophile label – well stick as much as I can given the moisture. I like being here in the Pacific Northwest surrounded by resilient sorts who know that every cloud has, if not a silver lining, another cloud behind it that is more a light heather than gray. Sorts who go out and smell the May flowers even if they get damp doing so. Who carry drying cloths to clean the raindrops off their sunglasses and who don't mind smelling like a wet dog. (Truth be known, I pick my friends by their ability to tolerate that specific aroma.)

And remember: eventually the flowers will bloom, the sun will shine, and we'll have three glorious months to celebrate the sights and sounds of road construction season.

**50 Shades of Gray Domestic Shorthair Cat**

If you desire a relationship with me, please read and sign this contract spelling out our roles and limits. As I've told you during our short time together already, the relationship spelled out in this contract is the only type I have and if you don't sign (and I really hope you do because I'm fascinated with you), we will have to go our separate ways.

CONTRACT

On this day _____, 20__ ("The Adoption Date")

BETWEEN

FELINE ("The Dominant") and HUMAN ("The Submissive")

The following are the terms of a binding contract between the Dominant and the Submissive.

**ROLES**

1. **The Submissive** is to serve and obey the Dominant in all things unhesitatingly and with enthusiasm. By signing this contract, she signifies that she:
   - Shall make herself available 24/7, or, better yet, 25/8. Yes, that means quitting her job, shunning her friends and family, and cutting off all other ties with the outside world. The Dominant is now her entire universe around whom she revolves.
   - Understands that despite what others may believe, she is now the property of the Dominant, not vice-versa.
   - Will keep herself healthy so that she has the strength and energy to meet every need, whim, desire, wish, fancy, or briefly entertained delusion of the Dominant.

- Accepts any and all disciplinary actions the Dominant considers necessary in order to keep her in line. These may include but are not limited to: clawing, scratching, flogging with the tail, meowing incessantly in the middle of the night, and pouncing on the head.
- Agrees never to look directly into the eyes of Dominant, nor attempt to brush his teeth no matter how horrid his breath may be.
- Will not bathe the Dominant; the Dominant is perfect as is.

2. **The Dominant** shall take no responsibility for anything, except for punishing The Submissive when she has failed to live up to her duties.

3. **The Dominant** has the right to ignore the Submissive at any time, but the Submissive is not to show hurt feelings or plot any kind of revenge.

## ACTIVITIES

4. The Submissive shall not participate in activities that take any time away from The Dominant. These include activities done in the house, for example, chatting with "people" on Facebook, playing Angry Birds, or staring out the window daydreaming.

## RULES

5.  The Submissive shall have no relationships with other humans or felines during the time the contract is in effect. (The fact that there will be no relationship with canines is a given and does not need to be spelled out here).

6.  All clothing worn by the Submissive should be comfortable for the Dominant to lounge on. Cotton t-shirts and sweat pants or flannel pajamas are preferred. No shoes are to be worn at any time unless they are fuzzy slippers, preferably shaped like mice.

7.  When interacting with the Dominant, the Submissive shall stay perfectly still at all times. The slightest movement, including laughing, coughing, or breathing too heavily, will displease the Dominant and result in punishment.

8.  The Submissive swears to get 20 hours of sleep per day, so that she is fully rested and able to meet the Dominant's need with the energy required. She may be awakened from sleep at any hour by the Dominant leaping upon her with claws fully extended, but must sleep when the Dominant chooses to take a catnap. However, she is not allowed the spot on the sofa or bed on which the sun shines during the day.

9.  Although the Dominant will regularly train the Submissive in the ways that bring him pleasure, the Submissive will never attempt to train the Dominant in any way.

10. A strict diet must be adhered to by the Submissive; that diet will include only foods that the Dominant enjoys eating and/or playing with. This list will be provided once the contract is signed and notarized.

11. The Submissive must exercise for three minutes every day in order to keep up with the Dominant.

12. Needless to say, smoking, use of alcohol or caffeine, or lighting candles or incense is prohibited. Only the Dominant may use drugs of any kind.

## SAFEWORDS

13. There are some demands the Dominant may make that the Submissive cannot meet without financial, physical, or emotional harm. In times such as this, the Submissive may make use of the safeword, "Fritz."

14. The Dominant shall ignore the safeword and expect the Submissive to meet his demands no matter the consequences.

## LIMITS

No neutering.

No acts involving loud noises.

No watching of television shows featuring dogs, even in minor roles.

No acts that will leave permanent marks on the skin in places that can be seen.

The following will happen only with consent: being bitten, foot pouncing, hair pulling, lap sitting until legs fall asleep, sand-paper tonguing.

## E-MAILS BETWEEN THE PARTIES

From: The Submissive
Subject: Isn't this contract a little over the top?

Can't we just have a normal human and cat relationship?

From: The Dominant
Subject: There is nothing normal about me

It's about time you acknowledge legally and irrevocably that I am in charge here and that you are all mine. If you don't want to be involved in this type of relationship, I advise you to steer clear of me. I am not the cat for you.

From: The Submissive
Subject: Sometimes I need to see other people and even other cats.

Even though you're bright and challenging, I need the intellectual stimulation of talking to people. Just to stay sane. And occasionally it would be nice to interact with other felines, not intimately, but just an occasional pat on the head or belly rub. Can we negotiate on this point?

From: The Dominant
Subject: There will be punishment

No. This is non-negotiable. You are mine (although I do like it when you beg.) I'm used to getting my own way. And remember, I can see in the dark and always know where you are.

From: The Submissive
Subject: Staying still

We both know I can't stay completely still. What if I have to pee? What if I'm choking on popcorn or a bee lands on my nose? Besides I like it when you move, why can't you enjoy me doing the same? I feel this is too restrictive and will prevent me from fully enjoying our time together.

From: The Dominant
Subject: I can teach you to be still

What you seem to fail to understand is how freeing complete surrender to my demands can be. I'm a good teacher—I can train you how to take shallow breaths so that when I sit on your lap your stomach doesn't go up and down and bother me. And you won't be eating popcorn as it is not on the approved list of foods, for the very reason you stated in your communiqué.

From: The Submissive
Subject: Motionless AND fat?

I really need more than 3 minutes of exercise a day or I'll balloon up. How about 30 minutes a day so that I can at least maintain enough muscle tone to lift you onto the top of the kitty condo? I'm only thinking of you and your needs.

From: The Dominant
Subject: Squishy is perfect

30 minutes of exercise is far too much. Your thighs could get muscular and that would not please me at all. I need you soft and comfortable like a down pillow only warmer and less likely to cause me to sneeze.

# Hey, Red!

There's something about a redhead. I may be biased, having been born red-headed and kept up the "tradition" thanks to boxes of hair color with names such as Copper Penny, Awesome Auburn, and Hey, Who Started the Fire?

What can I say, I love redheads. My first dog Copper was a "ginger" as we're often called these days. (By the way, ginger is also my favorite spice.) Three of my best friends have had fiery hair and dispositions, as did my favorite high school and college teachers. I wanted to be Julie Andrews in 1965 when The Sound of Music Came Out, I loved Lucy in reruns in high school, and in college I once fashioned a Halloween costume out of a kitchen rod and curtain in homage to Carol Burnett's classic "Went with the Wind" sketch.

Needless to say, when I was invited to not only attend Carol Burnett's recent show, I did my best Tarzan yell (at home to my dogs who don't judge me because I'm the only one tall enough to get them cookies) and immediately accepted. When I found out I'd also get to meet one of my red-headed childhood icons, well, there may have been some drinking at an inappropriate hour of the day, but I'll deny it if questioned.

I am not celebrity-crazed. Generally, when people ask me who my favorite actor, comedian, athlete, etc., is, I'll truthfully name someone I know personally. I don't cyber-stalk stars nor do I make them my friends on Facebook. But there are a handful of people whose remarkable talent is underscored by compassion, honesty, and class, and Carol Burnett is one of those people to me. And of course, there's the hair color – which, by the way looked fantastic under the spotlight. (That's another reason I love redheads. We don't shy away from the spotlight because it sets off our flaming coifs. We do, however, shy away from sunlight.)

There was something special about the type of comedy Carol represents(I know she would be okay with me using her first name because last night someone addressed her as Ms. Burnett and she responded with

"Call me Carol.") Hers was sketch comedy that wasn't mean-spirited or snarky, that allowed everyone's talents to shine, and in which it was clear everyone was having the time of her or his life. It was playful and silly and took risks in ways that didn't have to push boundaries of profanity or sex. I wish there was more of that in today's comedy offerings. No, I'm not an old fuddy-duddy – I can and will laugh with harder-edged comedy, but I miss the kind of sheer joy that shone through every Saturday (and then Sunday) night from 1967 until 1978. Ellen DeGeneres and Jimmy Fallon are working hard to bring that kind of fun-loving comedy back.

Carol's show was a night of questions and answers, just like what she did long ago on TV. I had three possible questions prepared. (1) What brand of hair color did she use and what shade? (2) Did she think Jerry Lewis was funny (this is in reference to the fact that Jerry has said more than once that he don't think women make good comedians. But what does he know, his hair isn't even red!)? and (3) In a society always looking for ways to prevent aging and look younger, did she think comedy was the fountain of youth? I had settled on questions #3 because at 81, Carol is still one hot tamale.

Unfortunately, I never got a chance to ask my question, but it didn't matter. The evening was laughter-filled and warm-hearted. Carol's stories were not only engaging, but the fact that she remembered so much at her age made me scratch "Get Gingko Biloba" onto my notepad while listening to her. Of course, I can't remember where I put that list…

During the questions, I discovered that Carol and I had more in common than just fake hair color. We were both nerdy girls, spent time living in Texas (she was born in San Antonio), and found our comedy calling accidentally. She wanted to be a cartoonist and had to take a theater class in college, which changed her path. I wanted to be a politician and decided if I were going to lie and exaggerate all the time, I'd rather do it while being funny.|

Backstage, I was introduced to her as "a local comedian and comedy writer." Wow, what a rush. And then Carol laughed at something I said. I'm not going to say I can die happy now because I want to live happily for a long, long time, but it was a good night. And I will admit that I'm staring at the wooden drapery rod in my office wondering if I should wear it to the drugstore to buy hair dye.

I so glad we had this time together.

## Dogmantics

Ever since cave dwellers fought over whether a sideways buffalo drawn on the wall meant "life's journey" or "party until the animals fall over," we humans have disagreed on exactly what our language mean.

For example, when I hear a supermodel says her 6" stiletto heels are *comfortable*, I know she does not define comfort the same way I do, i.e. "wearing sweat pants and bunny slippers while sipping hot vegan cocoa on the sofa with three dachshunds sleeping on my stomach." When a foodie describes a 1" in diameter stack of quinoa and kale as a *meal,* I know we not only differ in our definitions, but also that we should never dine together. And despite my preconceived notions of the true meaning of the word *study*, my UO students think it means "to listen to Taylor Swift sing about love gone wrong while scrolling through Tinder for possible dates, all in the vicinity of an open textbook."

Perhaps the way we use words reflects our life experience more than what dictionaries and thesauri dictate. By the way, isn't *thesauri* a great word? The mind conjures up a small dinosaur with thick glasses who enjoyed hanging out in the library. Kind of like me as a child.

As a dog mother for the past 31 years (that's 237 in dog years and 12 in middle-aged person years), I have found that even though I and my dogless friends and acquaintances use similar words and phrases, we're usually talking about things that are altogether different.

For example, the other day I said to a man who knows me, but not my family: "Justin, my 16-year-old, has dementia." After a loud gasp and a look that clearly indicated that he was thinking, "How can you tell if a teenager has dementia? None of them remember anything," it became clear that this guy mistakenly thought that I was talking about a human child.

After clarifying, I believe I saw him roll his eyes at me. How dare I imply that my son was ill when it was "just" my dog? And yes, I understand there are differences between raising a human and canine child. For example, mothers of human children get to potty train their kids in the comfort of a warm house while we dog moms often spend hours outside in the rain muttering, "I'll give you a big cookie if you finish your business in the next minute." *Business* is another word that has a different meaning in dogmantics (the language of those whose lives revolve around hounds). So is *failing*. When your child fails a class, chances are it wasn't because she chased someone around a gym while barking and baring her teeth. And if it is, perhaps you should have her tested for distemper.

When I first started down the road to crazy dog mom territory (take a right at the sign covered in hair), there were far fewer people who considered animals part of their families. Dogs, cats, hamsters, rabbits, fish, etc. were called "pets" (the same word we used back then to mean "making out," which really confused me when I was young). They were not allowed in the house, much less on the furniture. People were considered "owners." Those were such dark times.

There are still folks who need to categorize family into real and step, birth and adopted, two-footed and "Ew, you let an animal kiss you on the lips?" To me *family* is anyone you'd want to spend your last days on earth with, no matter their species or blood connection.

In an effort to get us all on the same page, here are a few other definitions from the language of dog parents:

Bad boy/bad girl – Human parent (HP): a kid who gets a tattoo or rides a motorcycle. Canine parent (CP): child who eats a new pair of shoes or the arms off the sofa.

Walk – HP: to traipse around the block while cajoling children to put down their electronic devices and look around at the real world for heaven's sake. CP: to stand in one place for half an hour while your dog sniffs every molecule of aroma from a tree, shrub, hydrant, curb, weed, or butterfly just in case there's a message they missed last time.

Birthday party – HP: annual event that involves dozens of screaming youngsters who smear cake and ice cream on every surface in exchange for a toy that will be broken before the party is over. CP: annual event at which mom or dad attempts to get child to wear a hat for even a few seconds so photos can be taken; there may also be cake, but it will be liver-flavored.

Time out – HP: giving a child the opportunity to reflect on his most recent transgression. CP: having a stiff drink because you deserve it and doing so doesn't set a bad example for your kids who frequently drink from the toilet.

Hey, maybe I should write the official human to canine parent translating dictionary. In the meantime, let's just all agree to disagree. Woof?

CPSIA information can be obtained
at www.ICGtesting.com
Printed in the USA
JSHW032056090721
16733JS00003B/119

9 781495 165115